Cover Design: Marie Taylor, TMG Taylor Made Graphics

www.tmgtaylormadegraphics.com.au

Pastured
Egg
Farming
Starting Out

Lee McCosker

ISBN: 978-1-326-93124-7

Because of the dynamic nature of the Internet, any web addresses or links contained in this book may have changed since publication and may no longer be valid. The opinions, advice and information contained in this book have not been provided at the request of any person but are offered by the author solely for informational purposes. While the information provided has been formulated in good faith, it should not be relied on as a substitute for professional advice. The author does not accept liability in respect of any action taken by any person in reliance on the content of this publication.

About the Author

Lee McCosker has been involved in the pastured free range industry for a long time and has been an active and passionate advocate for this style of farming. She is the author of several pastured pig farming books and the CEO of PROOF – Pasture Raised On Open Fields.

While pigs have been the focus, poultry have always been a side line and a great interest, so much so, that Lee expanded her knowledge of egg production by completing Poultry Production and Poultry Nutrition Science at the University of New England.

This book is a combination of personal experience, knowledge gleaned from other producers, advocacy for free range farmers and where ever necessary, reference to good, sound science.

Contents

Introduction

This book is an introduction to the business of farming pastured eggs for profit. Its aim is to not only arm you with all the 'must do's', but to give you a clear understanding of *why* the must do's are so important. Knowing how things work and why they do puts you in the driver's seat and better able to steer your new business towards becoming a highly productive farm with the best outcomes for the welfare and health of your hens and that means, a healthy bottom line.

Pastured egg farming can be very rewarding and quickly turn a profit when you are equipped with the right knowledge and prepared for what is ahead. It's not much use being told that you just need to feed then hens a certain percentage of protein, that you will get so many eggs per day, that you just need to clean, grade, package and deliver your eggs, birds are usually vaccinated and that you will need to replace your flock every so often, if you don't know why. It is just as important to know what can go wrong and how to rectify and prevent it, and that is the purpose of this book. We want you to be successful and build a respected brand that is here for the long term, not just until the first problem occurs in the flock!

It is NOT the aim of this book to sell you any 'fluff' so it won't be full of hype and sales pitches, just experience, knowledge and when necessary, good old fashioned science to back up what you are reading.

What are Pastured Eggs?

If you have been researching the egg industry or following consumer trends, you will know that there has been a debate over what a free range egg is for a very long time. The demand for ethically raised chickens and eggs rose so dramatically that the large corporations also wanted a piece of the pie but weren't prepared to put as much effort as smaller operators had been into producing them. Instead they have applied the usual 'intensive' practices that has been the norm within the industry for some time.

In Australia, the definition of a free range egg has now been established and the outcome has been disappointing for both producers and consumers. The long battle over who gets to put the words free range on their egg carton, and the new 'information standard' that does not require the hens to actually go outside, has damaged the integrity of the term to the extent that genuine free range farmers have distanced themselves and now call their eggs Pastured. Pastured better defines the production system that free range was originally based on and meets consumer expectations for ethically raised hens.

The PROOF (Pasture Raised On Open Fields) definition of pastured is:

*All animals are born and raised outdoors with continuous and unconfined access to pasture throughout their life time. They are kept at a stocking intensity that will ensure forage is always available in a sustainably managed rotational grazing system.**

**with the exception of very young poultry that are not yet sufficiently feathered and poultry that must be protected from predation at night.*

It is important to point out that we do not call our eggs pasture fed. This could be viewed as misleading as it is not possible to raised chickens on a diet of pasture alone. This will be discussed further under nutrition. Describing your eggs as pastured defines the production system and not just what the animal is fed and this is a very important distinction to make if you want to steer clear of tangles with consumer laws.

So then, how do we define pasture?

Pasture is generally defined as land covered with grass and other low plants suitable for grazing animals. While we too often see egg producers promote themselves with pictures of hens on rolling green hills, this is often unrealistic especially in a country like Australia. Pastures are green at certain times of the year, but often, they are dry and therefore browned off. They are still pastures! We just need to be a little more honest in our marketing to avoid making misleading claims.

The Egg Market

Pastured egg production (including free range and organic) is increasing its share of the market at a very steady rate and the trend is set to continue as people become more informed about how their food is produced. These consumers want to feel good about the food they buy; that it is healthy for them and their family and that it was produced sustainably without any animal cruelty.

The majority of eggs are sold through major supermarkets. Unless you are a very large producer, supermarkets are generally not interested in small, boutique suppliers. Fortunately, green grocers, providores, butchers, smaller supermarket chains and whole food outlets are and they need product to give them a point of difference. This does mean that you will need to develop your own market unless you plan to sell to another branded trader. Farmers Markets are another option to explore.

As you can see in the Egg Industry Overview following, pastured, organic and other types have been classified as specialty eggs and produced in much smaller volumes than the now corporate 'intensive' free range category.

Egg Industry Overview
(as at 30 Jun 2016)

State flock percentage as at June 2014: (Source: ABS, cat. no 7121)	NSW/ACT: Queensland: Victoria:	31% 29% 24%	WA: SA/NT: Tasmania:	8% 7% 2%
Number of egg farms: (Source: ABS, cat. no. 7121)	252 – as at June, 2014			
Gross value of egg production (wholesale equivalent): (Source: ABARES)	A$724.4m – 2015/16 FY			
Egg consumption: (Source: AECL)	226 eggs per capita (MAT) – 2016 FY 224 eggs per capita (spot) – as at July, 2016			
Grocery egg sales value: (Source: IRI AZTEC)	$880.8 – 2016 CY			
Grocery egg sales volume: (Source: IRI AZTEC)	207.6 dozen – 2016 CY			
Grocery sales farming system market share: – June 2016 (Source: IRI AZTEC)	Cage eggs Free Range eggs Barn-Laid eggs Specialty eggs	volume 49.5% 40.7% 8.5% 1.3%	value 37.3% 50.6% 9.2% 2%	
Grocery egg price (average): – June 2016 (Source: IRI AZTEC)	Cage eggs: Free Range eggs: Barn-Laid eggs: Specialty eggs:	$3.24 per dozen $5.40 per dozen $4.68 per dozen $9.24 per dozen		
Grocery sales branding market share: – June 2016 (Source: IRI AZTEC)	Private-label/generic labels Proprietary labels	volume 57.5% 42.5%	value 47.5% 52.5%	
Egg product exports: (FOB equivalent) 2016 CY (Source: ABS)	Includes fresh, dried, preserved sweetened and albumin.	value A$3m		
Egg product imports: (CIF equivalent) 2016 CY (Source: ABS)	Includes fresh, dried, preserved sweetened and albumin.	value A$21m		

CY = Calendar Year (Jan to Dec)	MAT = Moving Annual Total	FOB = Free On Board	m = million
FY = Fiscal Year (Jul to Jun)	p = preliminary	CIF = Cost Insurance Freight	mt = metric tonne
b = billion	A$ = Australian dollars	g = grams	% = percent

Source: Australian Egg Corporation – Annual Report 2016

What you need to know before you get started

A move to the country, a carefree lifestyle free of the stresses of a hectic professional life and to finally be your own boss? Producing ethical, wholesome food to feed your family while supporting your passion for a sustainable world; sounds grand doesn't it? There are a few things you need to know before you pack up your life in the city and head for greener pastures.

- A flock of commercial layer hens lay eggs 7 days a week
- This flock will need your attention 7 days a week
- Layer hens need a nutritionally balanced feed 7 days a week
- Your flock needs to be protected from predators like foxes, wild dogs, eagles, quolls etc.
- The flock can develop behavioural problems like feather pecking or cannibalism if they are stressed, nutrition is incorrect, there are lighting problems or the birds are overcrowded
- Pastured hens may not produce as many eggs as those housed indoors
- Hens roaming freely outdoors could be exposed to disease in that environment
- Hens do go 'off the lay' for many reasons
- Hens can be very hard on the environment and destroy pastures if they are not managed correctly
- You will most likely need a License to operate
- You need to be aware of animal welfare codes of practice, food safety requirements and legal requirements for grading, packing, storing and handling of eggs
- You need to do your research properly and make sure you have the right land zoning, council approvals etc. Your neighbours may not be as keen as you are about pastured chooks
- Weather extremes can take their toll on hen health and increase mortalities
- The productive life of a hen is relatively short and you will be faced with having to cull your flocks
- You will need to develop you own market and be able to negotiate the best price for your eggs

Model Code of Practice for the Welfare of Animals – Domestic Poultry 4th edition

This model code is currently under review and the revised edition should come into effect by the end of 2017. This is a set of guidelines at present but the standards within the code will eventually become law. No doubt we will have to make substantial changes to this book and our course when it comes into force. We do predict that the major change will be around the free range definition and stocking rates for hens outdoors.

At present, there is little mention of what defines a free range system within the code, hence all the arguments that have consumed the industry for the past couple of years. The model code simply defines free range as (non cage systems) "Birds in free range systems are housed in sheds and have access to an outdoor range." There is also a requirement for outdoor hens to be stocked at less than 1500 birds per hectare but this has been superseded by the new definition and information standard. 10,000 hens per hectare is now the permissible stocking density.

Currently, only three production systems are described in the model code: cage, barn and free range. The latter two also being defined as non cage systems. When applying this code to a pastured egg farm the free range requirements will apply until any such time as the definitions are changed or new categories are added to the code. Don't let these defined production systems cause confusion about how you label your eggs. This is an animal welfare standard only and has nothing to do with how you package or market your eggs. We will discuss the legalities of labelling as Pastured in another section.

What you do need to know about the model code is that it sets out the guidelines for hen welfare for all producers, not just free range or pastured.

The code is intended as a guide for people responsible for the welfare and husbandry of domestic poultry. It recognises that the basic requirements for welfare of poultry is a husbandry system appropriate to their physiological and behavioural needs.

The basic needs of poultry are:

- Readily accessible food and water to maintain health and vigour;
- Freedom to move, stand, turn around, stretch, sit and lie down;
- Visual contact with other members of the species;
- Accommodation which provides protection from the weather and which neither harms nor causes distress;
- Prevention of disease, injury and vice, and their rapid treatment should they occur.

The principles of the 'five freedoms' apply to the model code:

- Freedom from hunger and thirst
- Freedom from discomfort
- Freedom from pain, injury and disease
- Freedom to express normal behaviour
- Freedom from fear and distress

Of course, we could all have a very different understanding of these freedoms but the model code is very literal in its application of them. Your idea of distress or discomfort may differ to how it is applied within the code. The model code is therefore the minimal requirements for animal welfare. As we know, there is a demand for higher welfare farming systems and that is where your market is. Your production system needs to set the bar higher to meet the needs of this market.

The PROOF licensing program bases its Guidelines on these Core Values:

- All animals* are able to range freely in open fields or paddocks
- Animals will not be kept in cages, stalls or crates
- All animals are kept at stocking densities that will ensure access to forage and grazing and; in the case of layer hens, shall not exceed 1,500 per hectare
- Densely confined production systems and feed lotting are not practiced
- All animals are able to interact with their herd or flock and to carry out natural behaviours

- All animals should thrive in their environment and not just cope with it
- All animals will be protected from predation
- Illness or injury will be addressed promptly so that no animal will be left to suffer
- Animals will be fed to meet their welfare needs as well as production requirements
- Surgical treatments that inflict unnecessary pain will not be performed
- There will be no use of growth promoters
- Pastured free range should be environmentally, economically and socially sustainable

*with the exception of very young poultry that are not yet sufficiently feathered and poultry that must be protected from predation at night.

These Core Values are further expanded in the PROOF Guidelines for Poultry

What is important in any independent Guidelines or Standards is that they must be underpinned by the model code and must not cause the producer to deviate from its basic welfare requirements.

The Model Code sets out standards for housing, space allowance (including sheds for free range hens), lighting, protection, food, water, inspections, health and disease, management practices, perches, litter, rearing and stocking densities. It is your responsibility as a producer to make yourself familiar with this code.

Common breaches of the Model Code

Most issues arise for producers when they are simply not aware that the model code exists, they have not familiarised themselves with it or they have purchased equipment or housing from a supplier that has not fully understood or applied the code to their product.

One area of concern is when purchasing some purpose built mobile hen houses or caravans. Please be aware that you **should not** be locking your hens in this type of housing overnight. Most do not meet the indoor space requirements for your hens. You must apply both the stocking density for hens when they are outdoors in the range, but also when they are housed at night. If your hens are locked in and cannot exit the structure, the indoor stocking densities must be applied. You cannot simply apply the requirement for perching either as the hens will not spend all the time they are enclosed on the perches and to force them to do so will be a serious breach of the model code. Water supply and shade and shelter are other areas of concern with these systems. Check with the manufacturer and get their written guarantee that their product is fully compliant with the code.

Knowing your market

Years of experience have shown us that the ideals of the well intentioned new comer to pastured production don't always quite fit with the realities of this industry. Dreams of your brand taking pride of place on the shelves of major supermarkets or having world renowned chefs expound the superior qualities of your product could be quickly quashed when you are faced with the commercial realities of this business. Understanding where your market is one of the most important first steps to take.

Who do you plan to sell to? Where do you plan to sell your eggs?

The answers to these simple questions will lay the foundation for the production practices you will put in place on your farm. As a boutique producer, you will most likely target specialty supermarkets, whole foods markets, green grocers, independent butchers, restaurants, cafes, health food stores and the like as well as farmer's markets. What are these people looking for? What do they expect your product to do for them?

No doubt your customers will be looking for transparency. They will want to know the story of your farm, have access to it through your website, Facebook page and brochures, and they will want assurances that your eggs meet their expectations for ethically raised, free roaming, pasture raised hens. Don't disappoint them, you rarely get a second chance.

Will keeping your hens stocked at 10,000 birds per hectare with no necessity for them to actually go outside satisfy these clients?

Strategic Planning

Your business plan is a blueprint for how your business will work and become profitable, your strategic plan is why all your plans are going to work - the reasoning behind it all.

The Strategic Plan needs to address:

- Your business' vision (what is your ideal?)
- What is your mission? (What do you want to do?)
- Who are your customers and what exactly do they want to buy?
- Who are your competitors and how do you compare with them?
- What drivers for change may affect what our customers want in the future?
- How will these driver impact on your competitors?
- Are you able to meet your customer's needs today while preparing for future change?
- What are you best at doing?
- Is everything you are doing aligned with your vision?

What are your goals?
- Short term (learn as much as possible about the pastured industry)
- Intermediate (develop a farm system that allows you to meet your vision)
- Long Range (develop a well known and respected brand)

SWOT Analysis.

- **Strengths** (marketing or industry experience, chef, selling ability etc.)

- **Weaknesses** (lack of knowledge of the industry, distance from market, don't like direct selling etc.)

- **Opportunities** (demand, networking with other producers, proximity to market)

- **Threats** (deceptive labelling, distance to markets, competition (accreditation could help), loss of trust in the term free range)

Formulate Your Strategy!

Getting Started

So, you have thought about your potential market and made some enquiries and you have a strategic plan. Right? A business plan is also highly recommended. For now we want to learn more about any council or planning requirements you may need, which breed of bird to choose, what housing and fencing will suit best, understanding feed inputs and what other infrastructure you may need. You need to think about all this before you can attempt your business plan.

Council Approval

Most agricultural enterprises do not need to seek council approval for their farm operation unless it is of an intensive nature. E.g. cattle feedlots. There are a couple of livestock operations that are generally classed as intensive by default. The two of note are pigs and poultry. There are good reasons for this although most pastured or extensive producers find it hard to reconcile. Pigs and poultry are not ruminants; therefore, they require feed inputs for production. While sheep and cattle are more recyclers of nutrient in pastures, your hens are going to be fed with feed being brought in to the property and the excess nutrient from that feed is going to be deposited into the paddocks that they graze. Obviously, if stocking rates are low this nutrient is going to take a long time to accumulate but if numbers are high, say 10,000 per hectare, the soil can become quite toxic within a short period of time and pose a risk to the environment. We will discuss pasture and soil management in another section.

Each state and local council will have different requirements so it is important the you find out what the requirements are for your land and what circumstances will trigger the need for a development application or other approvals. Seek out your councils Local Environmental Plan (LEP) for guidance. Poultry can be referred to as a livestock feeding establishment, intensive agriculture or intensive livestock keeping depending on your state. The LEP will contain a section that spells out the definitions. You are likely to read a definition for intensive agriculture as something like this one, "where animals are fed wholly or substantially on prepared or manufactured feed". Trying to prove that your very productive hens are fed wholly or substantially on pasture is impossible in a viable, commercial situation therefore you could not be classed as extensive agriculture.

You will need to have the right land zoning to farm poultry on a commercial scale and this can be found under the definition of each zone e.g. RU1 on the planning section of your council website or ring and ask. While agriculture is generally permitted without consent in rural zones, intensive agriculture is not. You need to know if you are going to be classified as intensive. Don't believe that because you are free range and outdoors that you are automatically classed as extensive. It will generally come down to the percentage of feed brought in to feed the animals. The council will also consider any natural water bodies or wetland on or near your land, if you are in a drinking water catchment, close to another poultry farm or if neighbouring homes are within proximity just to name a few. It will be a costly mistake to set up your poultry business without seeking the necessary approvals or getting some written assurance from the council that none are needed.

If a development application is necessary, Council will most likely require that you supply a Statement of Environmental Effect with your application.

A Statement of Environmental Effect (SEE) outlines:

- the likely environmental impacts of the development;
- how the environmental impacts of the development have been identified; and
- the steps that will be taken to protect the environment or to lessen the expected harm to the environment.

Council must consider a number of statutory matters when determining your application. These may include:

- The provisions of any environmental planning instrument (state environmental policies (SEPP's) regional environmental plans (REP's), and local environmental plans (LEP's));
- The provisions of any draft environmental planning instrument (that is or has been placed on public exhibition);
- Any development control plans (DCP's);

- The likely impacts of the development (including environmental impacts on both the natural and built environments, and social economic impacts in the locality;
- The suitability of the site for the development;
- Any submissions made; and
- The public interest.

What information must a SEE include?

- A SEE should be a written statement clearly titled 'Statement of Environmental Effects'. It should give an understanding of the thinking behind your development and includes information about the development that cannot be shown on the plans. The SEE should address, at minimum, the matters described below. If you think something is not applicable to your application, state why this is the case. The amount of information required will depend on the type and scale of your application and will include:
- A description of the site and surrounding locality
- Present and previous uses of the site
- Existing structures on the land
- A detailed description of the proposal
- Operational and management details
- Reference to any environmental planning instruments (state environmental planning policies, regional environmental plans, local environmental plans – including the zoning of the land) that are applicable
- Reference to any draft environmental planning instruments (that are or have been placed on public exhibition) that are applicable
- Reference to any development control plans that are applicable.

Site Selection

As we have previously discussed, check with your local council about land zoning and planning requirements first. You will need enough land to allows for adequate buffer zones between your operation and your neighbours. The site should be well drained and only gently sloping to flat. Without drainage, the soil will quickly become boggy and odorous and conducive to disease.

The land does not need to be very fertile because the advantage of pastured production is the improvements to soil that can be made when the environment is managed well. Be aware that nutrient inputs from hen manure may have a negative effect on some trees, particularly natives.

The model code approaches land management from an animal welfare perspective. The code states that the outdoor range should be sited and managed to avoid muddy or unsuitable conditions and if such conditions should develop, remedial action should be undertaken to rectify the problem. Poultry should not be kept on land that has become contaminated with poisonous plants, chemicals or organisms which cause or carry disease that could affect the health of the birds.

The Hens

There are many different breeds of poultry, their suitability to commercial egg production however narrows down your choice considerably. Many of the older breeds (and the more attractive ones) are what could be called dual purpose birds because they produce both meat and eggs. The lay rate of these birds makes them unsuitable as a viable option for a profitable egg producer. As poultry have become more domesticated, they have been selectively bred for traits that suit the relevant type of production – meat or eggs. It's a bit like the difference between dairy cows and beef cattle: a very different body conformation and genetic make up that has one partition their energy into producing milk but the other to meat.

The difference between a commercial layer hen and a meat chicken are now very distinct, there are however a few options when it comes to selecting the right layer hen for your business. The modern and highly productive strains of layers perform exceptionally well but they do require specialist nutrition and excellent husbandry and are capable of producing over 300 eggs per year.

The key changes in modern layer hens are:

- Earlier onset of lay
- Increased egg weight
- Improved feed efficiency

The modern hybrid layer has many great attributes. Apart from having the ability to lay a lot of eggs under the right conditions, negative traits such as broodiness have all but disappeared. These birds have until recent times been bred specifically for caged systems. This meant that problems developed for outdoor producers when diet, lighting, stocking densities etc. differed from a production system that restricted the birds access to each other. Aggression, feather pecking and cannibalism became a problem in many of the commercial hen lines. While poultry breeders have worked to produce a more suitable hen for outdoor conditions, you must do your homework and choose the right breed for your operation.

Commercial genotypes of layer hens are supplied by only a small number of breeding companies. These birds are the result of decades of careful selection and improvement. There is not much more room for improvement in these birds so achieving potential productivity is now dependent of nutrition, housing, husbandry and health care and sound management. Nutrition will account for around 60 – 70% of your cost of production so getting it right is very important. Refer to the section on nutrition.

There are several strains of highly productive layer birds available. These birds are predominantly hybrid cross breeds such as the Hy-line Brown, Isa Brown, Hisex Brown, Bond (Lohman) Brown, Bond Black and the Nulkaba Brown. A report published by the Australian Egg Corporation indicated that the Hyline Brown and the Isa Brown performed best in free range conditions (Nagle, Singh, & Trappett, 2005). However, the report also determined that mortality rates in all strains studied were unacceptable but decreased dramatically after beak trimming. The report concluded that further research into the nutritional requirements of free range birds was necessary. Other studies have indicated that better management practices such lower stocking rates, the ability to dust bathe, forage and escape confrontation can lead to management of such mortalities (Lay Jr, et al., 2011, Tauson, 2005). It would be worth investigation the more independent breeder, Nulkaba Hatchery.

The following information is from the breeders' websites and is not an endorsement of any particular breed:

The Hy-Line Brown
Benefits include superior feed conversion, liveability and egg production.

The eggs have superior shell colour, robustness, size and internal quality.

The Hy-Line Brown also has an excellent temperament making it ideal for both intensive and free-range environments.

Key features of the Hy-Line Brown are:

- The world's most balanced egg layer, producing over 350 eggs to 80 weeks, peaking in the high 90s
- Early laying age with optimum egg size
- Very economical feed consumption
- Best interior egg quality in the market.

The breed is constantly being improved, with each new Hy-Line generation representing the latest advancements in breeding technology and is bred for a longer, more productive life.

The Hy-Line Brown hen is also ideally suited to free-range applications. The calm temperament, excellent feather retention, robust egg shells and persistent production to 80 weeks make it a perfect choice for free range environments.

For more information download our Hy-Line Brown management guide

http://www.specialisedbreeders.com.au/the-hy-line-brown/

The Nulkaba Hatchery
Breeding programmes designed for barn and free range environment

Our genetic programmes are specifically designed to produce high performance livestock for the barn and free range environment. In addition to improving our poultry for the usual economic characteristics (egg production, egg size, etc. in layers and growth rate, feed efficiency, etc. in ducks and quail) we also pay particular attention to behavioural characteristics and broodiness. Increasing the prevalence of favourable behaviour patterns and reducing the incidence of broodiness results in easier flock management and improved economic performance in the barn and free range environment.

Heat tolerant livestock

Because our layer lines, our ducks and our game birds, have all been bred in Australia for consecutive generations in sheds that are not environmentally controlled, they have become adapted to the Australian environment and are now heat tolerant. This is in stark contrast to the regularly imported stock marketed by other breeding companies which is not specifically adapted to the environment experienced in the barn and free range production systems.

No beak trimming is required

Both our commercial broiler and our commercial layer are of a quiet and friendly (but not timid) temperament with no significant vices apparent. Because of this quiet temperament, no beak trimming is required for trouble free lifetime production. Beak trimming is of increasing concern to welfare lobbyists and minimising or avoiding this practice through improved behavioural characteristics will become increasingly important.

http://poultryonline.com.au/nulkaba-hatchery

The ISA Brown

The ISA Brown is a hybrid type of Sex Link chicken, Is thought to originally been the result of crossing Rhode Island Reds and Rhode Island Whites, but now contains genes from a wide range of breeds, the list of which is a closely guarded secret. The a ISA Brown is a hybrid, not a true breed, developed by breeding unrelated "dam" and "sire" lines together until the final ISA Brown result. It is known for its high egg production of approximately 300 eggs per hen in the first year of laying.

http://www.baiada.com.au

The Lohmann (Bond) Brown

Lohmann Brown is a market leader in the Australian Layer Industry supported by the breeding company Lohmann Tierzucht, based in Germany, who have over 50 years experience in breeding egg laying hens.

Lohmann Tierzucht has developed a unique range of layer strains to suit various production systems and market demands. The Lohmann Brown Classic which is available through Specialised Breeders Australia is the market leader for:

- Shell strength
- Shell colour
- Mild Temperament
- High Productivity

http://www.bondenterprises.com.au/website/wp-content/uploads/2015/03/Bond-Brown-Booklet-V2.pdf

Brown shelled or white shelled egg producers?

In Australia, it has become accepted that our eggs have brown shells. In many other parts of the world the opposite applies and they produce white shelled eggs. Is there any difference is egg quality? Not really. White eggs are produced by white (sometimes black) feathered chickens with light coloured earlobes while the brown eggs are laid by brown feathered chickens with red earlobes.

Day old chicks or point of lay pullets?

These are your two options for purchasing or replacing your flock. Day old chicks need to be well bred, free of disease and vaccinated before you buy them. Not vaccinating chicks from a commercial hatchery is not an option. The chick hatches into a sterile environment and is therefore extremely susceptible to any disease that it is introduced to once it enters a new environment. We cover this in more depth in our disease management section.

Rearing day old chicks requires attention to detail if the bird is to achieve its weight for age standard with sound conformation and bone strength. There can be many mortalities, especially in the first few days, when raising chicks and this needs to be considered when planning on how to build your flock. The use of artificial lighting and heating will be very necessary during the early weeks of rearing and nutrition management and recording will need to be precise for the best outcomes for the bird and your long-term profitability. While you may want to do things more 'naturally' and not use any mechanical aids, think about how long a hen broods her chicks in a natural situation. She keeps them under her wings and feathers to keep the dry and warm for weeks. She teaches them to scratch for food and what to eat. Always think about what an animal or bird would do in natural setting and mimic that the best you can. The husbandry of your young birds at this early stage is vital to achieve good growth and peak production throughout the bird's life. Any growth checks at this stage could permanently reduce production so understanding the nutritional requirements of your birds is paramount. Refer to section on Rearing Your Own Birds.

The temperature of your rearing facility can be gradually dropped after about 6 weeks of age to help acclimatise the birds to an outdoor environment. This will help eliminate stress when they are moved to their new housing. Don't forget to also include perches at all different levels in the rearing area to teach your hens how to perch, fly and jump from an early age. Access to sunlight is also important for birds that are going to spend their lives outside.

Point of lay pullets are young hens that are almost ready to start laying. This is the most reliable way to buy your flock but the most expensive. The birds have already gone through the problem stage of rearing and should be fully vaccinated. Within weeks you will be producing eggs!

There can be some issue with point of lays if they have not been acclimatised or introduced to perches before arriving on farm. You may have to teach them to climb perches, as ridiculous as that may sound. They will also suffer more stress in their new environment so introducing them gently and quietly is critical. Don't make any big changes to their diet. Try to feed them the same as they were receiving at the rearing facility until they are settled.

When chickens are confined to a shed be aware that sudden fright can cause them to flee in an attempt to escape and they can pile on top of one another in a corner and smother each other. This can occur in chicks, pullet or mature hens. Fright can be caused simply by slamming a door or having children run amongst the birds.

Housing

There are many options for hen housing from DIY to an array of purpose built caravans and mobile sheds. Do your homework and take your time to make a decision and do not get caught up in the sales pitch for some ready-made models. Contact farmers that are using any particular brand that has taken your fancy and ask them if they would recommend them. Many people are being sold on the ready-made business model without any real understanding of the egg industry and what it entails. The figures may look good on paper but what happens if your lay rate drops? Would you know why your hens have decided not to lay as much or the quality of your eggs has dropped or your egg shells are distorted or thin and unsalable? The number of eggs laid is not consistent throughout the laying cycle. It will fluctuate and without precise management and a sound understanding of layer hen nutrition and disease management, could fall so low that it could send you broke. The lay rate is an average of eggs laid per day over the entire laying cycle. There is so much more to running a pastured egg business that dropping a shed in the paddock even if it comes complete with feeders, roll away nest boxes, watering systems, solar power etc. etc.

A big selling point of ready-made sheds is roll away nest boxes with egg collection conveyor belt. These units can be purchased and installed in any shed. Take a look at companies like Bellsouth www.bellsouth.com.au There are many models available from single nest boxes to commercial setups. These systems do help keep eggs clean and eliminate a lot of time consuming and risky washing.

The Model Code of Practice for the Welfare of Animals – Domestic Poultry (model code) offers standards and guidelines for housing of all poultry including layer hens with minimal acceptable housing standards including stocking densities in Appendix 1 and 2.

In general, the model code states that floors, other surfaces, fittings and equipment must be designed, constructed and maintained to minimise the risk of injury and disease, and to adequately support the birds. For non-cage systems, the floor in indoor areas may consist of litter and/or slatted flooring, or wire flooring. When litter is used it must be managed well for the welfare of the hens.

In practice, most pastured egg producers use mobile housing systems that house individual, small flocks of birds. Industrial scale fixed shedding is not a good partner for pastured systems because they cannot be moved, therefore that hens cannot be rotated around the paddocks to manage pasture growth and soil health or the overloading of nutrient in the soil surrounding the sheds.

Mobile housing does not have to be elaborate and expensive. A shed structure on skids will suffice. What is important to know is that there are requirements within the model code for floor space and perch space per hen, nest boxes as well as the need for light and ventilation and access to food and water. You need to research and consider all of these elements in your housing design. Note: floor space specifications in any non-cage system may include any slatted or metal mesh areas and any areas occupied by feeding and watering equipment and nest boxes. Perching areas are not included.

Outdoor hens tend to get the feet dirty especially in wet conditions. This needs careful consideration when placing the nest boxes within the shed. Ready access without the opportunity for the feet to be dried somewhat will

20

mean a lot of soiled eggs. Dark corners in sheds can also encourage hens to lay their eggs on the floor especially if there are not enough nest boxes available.

Mobile housing of up to 1,000 hens has proven quite successful on many pastured egg farms. Larger units become too heavy to move and can only be relocated on very flat terrain. Hens are also more comfortable with the smaller flock sizes these sheds offer so stress levels are low and so are antisocial behaviours and aggression.

Fencing

A note on electric mesh fencing (as illustrated in the photo following). This form of internal fencing is great for keeping hens from straying and managing grazing of pastures. Take care to ensure that the stocking density in the range area available meets the guidelines of any farm accreditation or any claims you make about your production system eg. 1,500 hens per hectare. If you confine the hens to one area even for the best reasons, you must still comply with any stated or mandatory stocking densities.

Boundary fences should aim to keep predators out and your hens in so, ideally they would be a well strained wire fence covered in chicken mesh. This is not always possible on a large farm, so at a minimum, the fence should keep out other livestock.

Picture courtesy of Sommerlad Poultry

Picture courtesy of Sommerlad Poultry

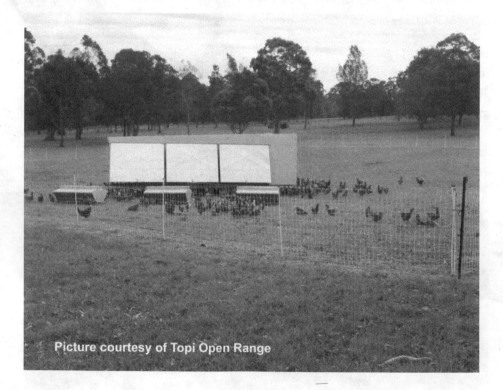

Picture courtesy of Topi Open Range

Perches and Nest Boxes

It is very natural for a hen to want to perch and often in quite a high position. After all, their ancestors perched in trees and your hens will to given half a chance. This is an instinctive behaviour and one that would protect them from night time predators and weather conditions. Hens that have been provided with perches during rearing will be more likely to use their nest boxes instead of laying eggs on the floor. You can also take advantage of this natural behaviour by making your perches higher than the next boxes to discourage birds from nesting in them at night and making a mess.

The current model code encourages the use of perches but does not make it a requirement. The PROOF guidelines require that all roosting birds have perches available to them.

The model code does state that when perches are provided they are to be linear with not less than 15 cm of space available for each bird. Perches must be without sharp edges and must be positioned to minimise fouling of any

23

birds below. The horizontal distance between the perches should be at least 30 cm but no more than one metre, and the horizontal distance between perch and the wall should be at least 20 cm.

Perches can be constructed of timber or metal and the ideal width is approximately 4cm to allow the hens to comfortably grasp it with their toes.

The model code states that laying hens must be provided with at least one single bird nest per 7 hens or, for colony nests, at least 1 m^2 of next box area per 120 hens. These are minimal requirements and to avoid problems with floor eggs or eggs laid outside in the grass, it may be advisable to provide more nest boxes. 5 hens per nest box would be less likely to cause problems with broken and dirty eggs. Colony nests are more likely to produce broken eggs simply because of the large volume of hens using it. 100 hens to each square metre of box area may be more applicable.

Nests must provide seclusion from the flock and be designed and have a floor substrate that encourages nesting behaviour. How the birds are reared will play an important role in ensuring that eggs are laid in the nests provided. Close off the nest boxes at night during the first week that the birds are moved to the layer housing. They will quickly learn to roost instead of getting into the boxes at night. If the birds were reared with perches, roosting behaviour should already be established.

Nest boxes and roosting areas should be easily accessible and should not be so high above the floor level that birds may be injured when ascending or descending. Graduated rails or perches can assist the hens to access and leave the nest boxes easily. The type of perch in front of the nest box is important and a 50 x 50mm rail is recommended.

If left to their own devices, hens will seek a dark and secluded spot to lay their eggs in. You need to make your nest boxes attractive to them as possible so consider this in your design. Hens like to scratch around and 'make a nest' so nesting materials should be made available unless you are using a roll away system. Litter also helps to keep the eggs clean and dry but must be managed well to do so.

Do not let direct sunlight on the nest boxes as this can be a cause of feather pecking. (see Feather Pecking)

Access to the Outdoor Range

You would now be aware that access to the range for free range hens is a very contentious issue. Unfortunately, in Australia, the wording setting out requirements in the model code has only ever referred to 'access' and made no clear stipulation that it was necessary for the birds to actually go outside to be classed as free range. While the Australian Competition and Consumer Commission (ACCC) initially took and different view and successfully prosecuted several so called free range producers based on consumer expectations, the new definition and information standard for free range has changed all that. The information standard makes it very clear that it is NOT necessary for hens to actually go outside on a free range farm, they just have to have 'meaningful' access to the outdoors.

PROOF has defined a pastured system as:

All animals are born and raised outdoors with continuous and unconfined access to pasture throughout their life time. They are kept at a stocking intensity that will ensure forage is always available in a sustainably managed rotational grazing system. *

The PROOF guidelines require that all birds are encouraged to spend time outdoors with adequate shade and shelter, easy access to water and feed and protection from real or perceived threat of predation. PROOF is an acronym for 'pasture raised on open fields', therefore it is expected that the majority of hens will use the range during daylight hours. Flock sizes must not exceed 2,500 birds in each and this also fosters a more harmonious environment for the hens and encourages the birds to go outside.

Allowing as much access as possible for entry and exit to hen housing will go a long way to encouraging the birds to go outside. Tiny pop holes or limited access can stop the hens from using them from fear of being bullied by others congregating at the exit, fear of injury if the exit is too high, fear of what is outside if they cannot see through easily, or simply because they cannot find the exit easily (in large sheds). Most pastured producers do not use inadequate pop holes, instead they have large doors or even entry under the shed. When free access is available for the birds and the environment is attractive to them with plenty of pasture, shade and shelter, the hens will use the range extensively. This access has the potential to be a marketing advantage for pastured producers.

The model code requires openings to the range to be a minimum of 35 cm high and 40 cm wide with 2 metres per 1,000 birds. This is very limited and would not encourage all birds to use the range, particularly in very large sheds. The code also requires that the birds have ready access to shade areas and shelter from rain, and windbreaks should be provided in exposed areas.

The PROOF guidelines encourage the planting of trees and shrubs for shade and protection for the birds. Sufficient exits from housing must enable ease of access for the birds to the range area. Exits will not contain barriers or structures that prevent or deter birds from exiting the housing.

Stocking Rates

If you are a relative newcomer to this industry you may not realise the significance of the 1,500 hens per hectare stocking rate that has dominated the debate over the definition of free range. Appendix 2 of the current model code sets out a stocking rate of a maximum of 1,500 layer hens per hectare. There was an argument mounted about a further section (that we believe applied only to meat birds) that allowed a proportionately higher stocking rate under certain conditions. Basically, the 1,500 hens per hectare was ignored by large producers and became a point of difference that defined genuine free range. This is all mute now though because the new definition has changed to 10,000 hens per hectare and this will be reflected in the upcoming revue of the model code.

As part of the new definition for free range, it will be a requirement that anyone labelling their eggs as free range also state their stocking rate on the carton.

The argument over free range has been long and protracted therefore consumers have become aware that 1,500 hens means something and for a while they will remember this. But for how long? When this requirement disappears from the model code in the very near future, will people forget or even question what the difference is if all cartons are labelled free range anyway? The other issue is, how many supermarkets will keep supplying eggs from 1,500 farms to keep awareness alive? If the only option is 10,000 hens per hectare will that become the new normal?

When it comes to stocking rates the environment should be your guide. Without healthy soils there will be no pasture and no pastured eggs! Don't lose sight of how all this began. It was driven by the consumer who has a picture in their mind of what an ethical, sustainable farm looks like and it does not include hens that rarely or never go outside or barren paddocks laden with chicken manure polluting the environment. In reality, most land can only carry around 750 hens per hectare (under optimal management) if it is to remain healthy and maintain pasture. Any higher rates are going to need excellent management skills.

The PROOF guidelines take an environmental approach to stocking rates although they are capped at 1,500 hens per hectare. The pastured definition within the guidelines requires that hens are kept at a stocking intensity that will ensure forage is always available in a sustainably managed rotational grazing system.

Water

Your hens are going to need a constant supply of fresh, cool and clean water. Water should be around 15ºC. This is most important during hot weather when the hens will access the water in an attempt to keep cool. Look at the water delivery system and keep pipes underground and not exposed to the sun. Black poly pipe can heat water to incredible temperatures and then birds will not be able to drink it.

Any old dam water will not do and any vessel used to supply water must be kept clean. The quality of your water can actually impact on the quality of your eggs. High levels of dissolved mineral can impact on egg shell quality and can be unattractive to the hens. Dirty water can impact on gut health or even invite disease.

Having a water supply outdoors is likely to attract unwanted birds and increase the risk of disease being introduced. Keep supply close to shelters to discourage unwanted visitors as much as possible. Avoid the use of large, open water troughs and use drinkers designed for chickens and not water fowl.

The model code requires that your hens have access to sufficient potable water that is cool in summer and maintained below a temperature at which the birds refuse to drink. The water must not be deleterious to health and there should be a minimum of one day's storage or auxiliary supply in case of breaks, repair or failure of pumping equipment. Each bird must have access to at least two independent drinking points.

Beak trimming and de-beaking

Here is another contentious issue for pastured producers. There is a very big difference between the laser trim given to day old chicks and cutting off the beak in older birds.

In an ideal situation with low stocking rates, stress free conditions, great housing, an interesting environment, the right breed of hen and sound nutrition, beak trimming of any kind would not be necessary. Problems do occur unfortunately but they should be investigated and rectified rather than relying on cutting off beaks. Many producers however are not given the opportunity because the hatchery they buy from trims all chicks and unless you are buying in big numbers, it can prove difficult to order or purchase birds with full beaks. There are more suppliers making non trimmed birds available. You will have to shop around and talk to other producers. We cover feather pecking in another section.

Protection from Predators

There are many potential predators when it comes to hens kept outdoors. Foxes are generally the main problem but local dogs (sometimes even your own dogs), quolls, goannas, snakes, eagles and hawks can all make protecting your flocks a real task.

Maremma dogs are used very successfully even on very large outdoor farms. Where they don't work is when people get too attached to them and hope to make them a dual-purpose animal – pet and guardian animal! They must bond with the flock if they are going to protect them. This doesn't mean you can't interact with the dogs, just don't try and make pets out of them.

Locking your birds up at night is an obvious solution for nocturnal pests such as the fox, but, if you are using housing that does not have sufficient floor space to comply with the model code requirements, this is not possible. Also, locking hens in at night also means that they must be let out very early in the morning so it can become a management issue.

We have had a lot of success with Foxlights in the past, even with our pig herd. The key is to use enough of them and follow the instructions. These economical lights come on at dusk and turn off at dawn automatically. They work on a totally random light display that predators are unable to predict. If you just put lights out at night, a fox would learn very quickly that it poses no threat. The only time that the Foxlights may be less effective is in built up areas were the foxes are used to seeing a lot of light, especially car headlights.

BATTERY FOXLIGHTS

The most advanced non-lethal method of night predator control.
A COMPUTERISED varying flash with 2 colours meaning predators are less likely to get used to.
Nine LED bulbs projecting at 360 degrees can be seen over 1 kilometre.
Set where stock are sleeping or near poultry pens. Foxlights appears as if someone is patrolling with a flash light which keeps predators away with their natural fear of man.
Operated with a six volt battery making it able to function in any location, shaded or not, and through all weather conditions.
The best battery will give 12 months of operation.
Easy set up on a steel fence post, hung from a tree or on an existing fence.
Easy to relocate with stock going to fresh pastures.
Foxlights is very compatible with all guard and domestic animals.

SOLAR FOXLIGHTS

The most advanced non-lethal method of night predator control.
A COMPUTERISED varying flash with 3 colours meaning predators are less likely to adapt to.
Nine LED bulbs projecting at 360 degrees can be seen over 1 kilometre.
Set where stock are sleeping or near poultry pens. Foxlights appears as if someone is patrolling with a flash light which keeps predators away with their natural fear of man.
A solar panel collecting energy stored in 2 AA rechargeable batteries. The life of these batteries should be 3 years. A USB port allows charging from mains if required.
Solar lights requires good sunlight and may not be suited for forested or shaded areas. We recommend a combination of both lights in some circumstances.
Easy set up on a steel fence post, hung from a tree or on an existing fence.
Easy to relocate with stock going to fresh pastures.
Foxlights is very compatible with all guard and domestic animals.

FOXLIGHTS ARE AN AID IN DETERRING NIGHT PREDATORS & MAY NOT PREVENT ALL ATTACKS.

Bird Management

Anyone that thinks they can put a caravan or shed of birds in the paddock, fill up the feeder and collect eggs once a day without much thought or input is sadly mistaken. Productive, profitable egg production is reliant on your management skills and attention to detail.

We hear all too often comments like 'if you have 100 hens you may as well have a 1,000', or, a producer starts out with 500 hens, demand is high so they order another flock of 2,000 hens thinking that a fivefold increase in numbers won't make much difference to an already established routine. What will happen is that if problems occur they will be multiplied five times!

- You must have the correct facilities to match the number of birds in your flock.
- Don't just consider the outdoor conditions for your hens. Night time accommodation and nesting areas are just as important.
- Don't mix new flocks with older birds or you are inviting diseases such as fowl cholera.
- Birds must be vaccinated.
- You must be aware of the possible diseases that could impact on your flock or production.
- Know what your production performance is. What is your lay rate? What is the mortality rate? These numbers aren't just about how you are doing, they can be triggers to investigate problems.
- Understand layer hen nutritional needs at different growth phases and what you are actually feeding your hens.
- Understand the changes in egg shell quality, egg quality and egg size through different ages and stages of a hen's productive life.
- Understand the impact grazing birds can have on the environment, not just the aesthetics, the damage to soil health and hen health.
- Keep good records and a farm diary.
- Be a good observer. Know what is normal in your flock so you can quickly see when something is not normal and investigate.

Rearing your own birds

There are two options for buying in flocks of birds; 'day old' chicks or point of lay pullets. We are going to step through the rearing of these birds from delivery on farm as chicks.

Definition of a pullet; young chicken between the age of 1 week and 18 weeks of age. The female layer pullet before sexual maturity. (before lay)

The goal of pullet rearing is simple; to optimise development during rearing for performance during the laying cycle.

Priorities:

- Establish good feeding behaviour
- Encourage a well developed digestive tract
- Uniformity within the flock (weight and size)
- Reaching body weight targets at specific age milestones

Key to good outcomes:

- Housing conditions
- Stocking densities
- Lighting
- Nutrition

Before the chicks arrive

Make sure you are prepared. You want the bird's transition to be as stress free as possible with minimal change and disruption.

- Clean up
- Eradicate insects
- Exterminate rodents
- Wash all equipment
- Disinfect the shed, caravan or shelters
- Rest for at least 10 days before repopulating

Ensure you have everything in place and in working order:

- Heat lamps
- Water
- Feed
- Bedding materials
- Perches
- Thermometers to monitor environment

Day old chicks from a commercial hatchery are usually vaccinated against Newcastle Disease, Marek's disease and Infectious Bronchitis. Ask what your chicks have been vaccinated against. It should be provided on your invoice. We will talk further about vaccinations and why they are so necessary.

Brooder Management

A brooder is simply a heated environment for young chicks, starts out small and expands with the growth of the birds.

It is very beneficial to surround the brooding area with a sheet of upright cardboard (usually corrugated), plywood or hay bales to exclude drafts and to confine the very young chicks to a smaller area so that they do not travel too far from their heat source or food and water. Depending on how many chicks you are rearing, the brooder may well start out as a cardboard box. The chicks will still need plenty of space to allow them to adjust the comfort levels and escape too much heat as well as investigating their environment. The brooder will also need bedding materials such as straw or wood savings to help keep it dry and clean.

It is essential that the young chicks have access to plenty of water and very fresh feed. Getting them eating quickly is vital. Use a chick crumble to get your birds started quickly. Spread heavy paper on the ground and sprinkle some feed over it in the first couple of days. The rustling noise it makes when the chicks peck or scratch at it attracts others. Do this near the main food source. For the first week, make water available in shallow dishes while the birds learn to use drip systems but keep it away from direct heat. There will usually be a percentage of 'non-starters' that will die because they just never learn to feed.

In the first couple of weeks minimise ventilation and think again about the conditions under the broody hen. Prevent air drafts and provide uniform temperature and humidity where possible.

Ideal temperatures in the brooder

This is a guide only and will be dependent upon the conditions under which you are rearing your birds. The suggestions below assume a purpose build shed is being used, that relative humidity is around 40 – 45% and that chicks are reared in the brooding area for six weeks. Depending up your climatic conditions, you may choose to let the chicks start wandering outdoors once they are sufficiently feathered and fully vaccinated (approx. 8 weeks).

Age of Pullet	Room temperature °C
Placement	34-36
1-2 days	34-32
3-4 days	31
5-7 days	30
7-14 days	28-29
14-21 days	26-27
21-28 days	22-24
28-35 days	18-20
35-42 days	18

A very gradual reduction in temperature mimics the natural conditions of the mother hen. In the beginning the chicks would be under her wings and feathers for most of the day where it is very warm and quite humid. As they quickly grow and start investigating their environment and learning to eat, they will spend less time under the hen during the day. As they grow larger it is harder for them to have the full protection of the hen. If conditions permit, you could start letting the birds venture outside at this stage. Slowly acclimatise your birds to the growing environment they will be introduced to. Raise heat lamps or use less of them to adjust temperatures. Of course, if it is very cold or hot, you must manage those conditions and supply appropriate protection such as air conditioning or roof sprinklers.

Have a vaccination program in place. The chicks should have arrived with initial vaccinations, it is your job to complete the program and ensure the health of these young birds. It is not advisable to allow the birds outdoors until their vaccinations are complete at approximately 8 weeks of age.

Pullet Nutrition

Feeding management is critical to the ultimate productivity of your grown pullets and late intervention is rarely successful. You can't catch up of you messed up! Pullets that are meeting target weight at maturity will be the best egg producers. It is that important that you feed your young birds properly. How do you know how much to feed and what the target weights are? Whatever breed of layer hen you have, you will find this information available on the breeder's website. There is generally a complete guide from rearing to end of lay.

Energy intake at this life stage appears to be the limiting factor for growth. Don't get too caught up in the crude protein percentage stated on feed bags and ignore the bird's requirements for energy. A deficiency of energy will show as slow or stunted growth and lowered production of eggs. Feed your birds according to body weight rather than according to their age.

Guidelines for the 4 phases of pullet growth (Poultry Hub, 2017)

Nutrient	Units		Starter 0 – 6 wks	Grower 6 – 12 wks	Developer 12 – 15 wks	Pre-Layer 15 wks – Prod.
Protein	%	Min	20.0	17.50	15.50	16.50
Metabolisable Energy	Mj/Kg		11.5-12.4	11.5-12.6	11.3-12.4	11.4-12.4
Metabolisable Energy	Kcal/Kg		2750-2970	2750-3025	2700-2970	2725-2980
	Kcal/Lb		1250-1350	1250-1370	1225-1350	1235-1350
Lysine	%	Min	1.10	0.90	0.66	0.80

There are four recognised phases of pullet growth: Starter, Grower, Developer and Pre-Lay. In the first ten weeks of life the pullet is not able to regulate its energy intake. 80 – 90% of its body frame will have developed by

8 weeks of age so it is important to maximize this time and take advantage of the potential to feed the high amounts of energy that can be encourage in the first 10 weeks. After this time there is no point to feeding extra energy because the frame has developed and excess energy will be laid down as fat.

Energy dense crumbed feed should be used at this stage instead of mash to encourage intake and maximize growth.

After the 10 week point, the pullet will adjust their feed intake to match their energy needs.

Lighting is necessary to grow your chicks to this stage to promote early development and sexual maturity. If chicks are kept in the dark they will not eat sufficient amount of food, so if growth is slow, look at hours of light the birds are exposed to. Feeding activity is directly related to daylight hours.

See Nutrition.

Training your birds

Yes, it is necessary to train your pullets as they grow. Training may begin with simply teaching them to eat or drink! It may be necessary to attract the chicks to food by mimicking the hen's natural behaviour and scratching through the feed with your finger, or using paper as discussed previously. Drinker nipples should be dripping so that they can see water. Dip chicks' beaks in water dishes to encourage them to drink if necessary.

Providing perches for your birds from a young age will help tremendously with their development. Hens will climb to great heights to find a safe roosting spot when they have the ability and facilities. Remember: their ancestors roosted in trees!

Simply put, perches will:

- Encourage the full development of leg and flight muscles
- Habituate jumping behaviour that will be necessary for nesting
- Reduce social stress by providing safe resting sites
- Improve feed and water consumption
- Increase the effective space within housing

The brooder is generally pretty devoid of natural light and pullets raised by commercial breeders are often kept in intensive style sheds. Gradually increase the natural light they are exposed to, especially once the birds have moved to the rearing area, in preparation for the life outdoors.

When pullets learn to climb perches at a young age and experience light from the sun, their transition to the layer house and the outdoors is much easier for them.

Moulting

Moulting is a natural cycle of feather loss and regrowth that is triggered by decreasing day length. When day light falls below 12 hours per day moulting may begin. You could artificially extend daylight hours by installing lights in the hen housing. Moulting is a time of rest and rejuvenation for the hen who, like all animals, was never meant to reproduce 12 months of the year. There are other contributing factors that will bring about a partial moult and they include stress, feed and water shortage, disease and sudden changes in exposure to light. A partial moult is usually seen as feather loss to the head and neck with perhaps some impact on egg production. During a full moult, egg production could cease almost completely. When you hear the term 'gone off the lay', it is generally in reference to the hens going through a moult.

Moulting usually occurs after 8 to 12 months of egg laying with high producers tending to be later than poorer performers. In a more natural pastured environment, this means that your flock may not all moult at the same time, instead you could experience a drop in egg production over a period of months. This is why some producers choose to cull their flocks at this age and start fresh with a new one and avoid the inevitable decrease in lay rate. If you have modelled your business plan on a set number of eggs to be produced each day, you will probably have little choice but to replace your flock early. You will have to weigh up the cost of flock replacement against reduced egg production.

Under intensive, housed systems, forced or controlled moulting may be practiced instead to extend the laying life of the hens. This involves the use of lighting programs and nutritional restrictions that force all hens to moult rapidly at around the same time.

Daylight and artificial light

As you have learned from the previous section, daylength and light have a huge influence on layer hens. Chickens are naturally programed to reproduce at certain times of the year and they recognise that by the length of daylight. It is a real challenge for the pastured producer because you have little control over how much light your hens are exposed to.

In a controlled, housed environment artificial lighting is used to control exposure and trick the hens biological system. Lighting programs are used to virtually mimic the season so that the hen thinks she has reached sexual maturity in spring.

Another problem arises if pullets are purchased from a supplier that does not adjust light exposure appropriately for birds that will live outdoors. You could find that the pullets you purchase came from a semi-dark house and will now be suddenly exposed to a huge amount of daylight with detriment effects on the lifetime productivity of the bird. To try and overcome this you could make sure your sheds or housing are not oriented towards the sun and that doors and windows are not fully extended at first. It will still be difficult to stop the effects of sudden exposure so try and purchase pullets from a breeder that understands where his birds will be sold to and has an appropriate lighting or daylight exposure program in place.

Culling the Flock

Reduced lay rates at the end of the lay cycle (prior to moulting) or age of the flock are the main reasons for culling birds. We have already discussed moulting above. Egg quality and lay rate declines with the age of the hen and while you may decide to take your flock through a moult, eventually the reduce number of eggs, changes in egg quality, shell quality and size of the egg will mean that the hens have to go.

It is probably the biggest deterrent to egg farming, having to kill or dispose of entire flocks of birds. On a smaller scale, you could offer your hens for sale to backyard growers because there are still plenty of eggs left in the hen, just not enough and of high enough quality to keep your business viable.

Because the birds roost at night and generally in a shed that can be closed, culling at night is recommended. The birds are less likely to be frightened or go off the lay if you are selling them. Even if you are just checking the flock for poor layers, night time is best so that it doesn't disrupt the rest of the

38

laying hens. You may want to investigate possible markets for spent hens such as welfare friendly pet meat.

Identifying non-laying hens

The health of the hen is reflected in her overall condition. The wattles and comb should be bright red and the head will be trim with bright eyes. The poor layer can be identified by a pale comb and wattles and dull eyes. The vent of a good layer will be smooth, large and moist the pubic bones having at least two fingers width between them. The abdomen should be deep and soft with little body fat and the measurement between the tip of the keel or breast bone and the pubic bones should be three or four fingers in width. Non-layers will usually have a smaller, firm body with only a depth of about two finger widths between the pubic bones and keel. The pubic bones are usually stiff and close together when the hen is not laying and the vent is small and puckered. (Mississippi State University Extension Service).

You will have noticed that the colour of your pullets before commencement of lay is quite different to a hen that has been laying for some time. The most noticeable is the colour of the legs which will be quite yellow in the pullet. As the pullet begins to lay, the yellow colour stored in her legs and other body parts is used to colour her egg yolks. The colour in her legs, beak, eye rings, feet, ear lobes and vent will disappear as the bird progresses through the lay cycle. Depending on the colour and breed of your flock it may not be as noticeable as some. When the hen ceases to lay the colour will return in the same order that it disappeared. Following is a guide:

Body Part	Time After First Egg
Vent	4-7 days
Eye Ring	7-10 days
Base of Beak	4-6 weeks
Tip of Beak	6-8 weeks
Bottom of Feet	8-10 weeks
Front of Shanks	15-18 weeks
Rear of Shanks	20-24 weeks
Hock Joint	about 24 weeks

(Mississippi State University Extension Service)

Feather pecking and other behaviours

Hearing and vision are the highly developed senses in the chicken and they play a crucial role is social behaviour, communication and response to predators. The chicken has 2.5 times more optic fibre in the optic nerve than humans and has approximately 300 degree vision. Because of the flatness of the eyeball, chickens tend to move their heads and neck when following an object. It is thought that hens do have colour vision. Hens also have very good hearing that is as sensitive as human hearing. (Scanes, et al., 2004)

There has been tremendous progress in the genetic selection of poultry for traits that improve productivity such as eggs laid per hen and feed conversion, but, it is not clear how adaptive, behavioural and phycological mechanisms have kept up. There is much more to a providing the best welfare outcomes for the chicken than just the essentials to ensure maximum production. Hens should be bred, raised and selected for adaption to their environment.

Pastured hens could spend at least half their day in the paddock foraging and feeding and that could result in around 14,000 individual pecks! Chickens peck their food while other poultry species scoop their food into their mouths. (Scanes, et al., 2004)

You must be familiar with the normal behaviours of your flock so that if a behavioural problem should erupt you can quickly spot it. The usual signs of good health and well behaved birds are alertness and eating.

Lay Jr, et al. (2011) suggest that feather pecking can become redirected foraging behaviour when factors such as diet, stress, disease and overcrowding reduce the opportunity for normal foraging behaviour.

Feather pecking can be the result of many different factors. Pecking and cannibalism can occur in free range birds and are usually the result of a problem in the management system such as when overcrowding occurs or when stress, disease and diet impact on the birds' ability to carry out normal foraging behaviour. The birds are driven to peck and we have already touched on this above. If all food is consumed quickly each day and there is no other stimulation in their environment, hens may peck one another. It may start out as inquisitive behaviour but it can escalate quickly. Hens are vulnerable to pecking straight after laying an egg because the cloaca is exposed for a brief moment and this attracts attention. For this reason you should not let direct sunlight into nesting boxes so that other hens can see this event clearly. Perches placed too close together can also encourage the hens behind to start pecking at the bird in front. Again it can start as an isolated event that then catches the attention of other birds.

Not all feather pecking is just misguided behaviour. Poor nutrition is often a major driver. As we discuss in nutrition, amino acids (building blocks of protein) must be supplied in the hens' diet and Methionine is the most limiting for laying hens. Methionine is needed to grow feathers so this will explain why a hen that is deficient would turn to pecking and eating feathers in an attempt to meet her nutritional needs.

Feather pecking and cannibalism can simply be the result of an unbalanced or protein deficient diet and the bird is driven into survival mode, or it could be that dead carcasses have not been collected from the paddock and birds have started to peck at them and decide to continue the behaviour.

Overcrowding however is the most common cause of feather pecking.

An environment that encourages exploration and caters to the inquisitive nature of the chickens, lower stocking rates and good nutrition will help to prevent feather pecking but should it occur all management practices should be reviewed to find the cause.

Nutrition

Whenever you are trying to sort through issues with pastured free range systems, go back to basics and think about how the birds would behave in its natural habitat. What is the natural habitat of a chicken?

Your chickens' ancestors were Gallus Gallus, the red jungle fowl, and they would have spent their days foraging and scratching around on the forest floor of native jungles of Asia and India. Their diet would have consisted of mainly of insects, worms, bugs, frogs as well as seeds, grasses and fallen fruits and berries.

Today our highly productive poultry are fed a diet that consists mainly of wheat, corn and soybean and it has become necessary to include all sorts of feed additives to balance out the birds' diets. You have probably heard of some of the more controversial additives like egg yolk colouring, Methionine or antibiotics. They are difficult to avoid when we are trying to produce a quality product and still keep production at sustainable levels. However, a more natural approach to feeding layer hens is possible when you better understand some of the basics of bird nutrition.

Chickens need a balanced diet that mimics what they would be eating if they had free choice – a mix of animal and vegetable proteins and it is very important to understand that no one feed ingredient alone will meet the bird's nutritional needs and feed additives like Methionine are used in the industry for a very valid reason – it is critical to egg and feather production. When you mix your own diet for your chickens you need to ensure that all the essential amino acids (especially Methionine) are supplied in natural form in feed ingredients.

Eggs are packed with good nutrition, we all know this, but do you ever stop to think about how it got there? Eggs will only be as nutritious as the feed you give your chickens so if you want wholesome eggs loaded with Omega 3, vitamins and minerals and produced with healthy shells then you need to feed your hens accordingly.

A nutrient is a substance supplied in the hen's diet to meet a specific requirement and needed to perform a function in the body. A deficiency of a nutrient may result in health problems, reduced productivity or even death.

A feed ingredient is a material used to provide a nutrient or several nutrients. It is not the ingredient that is most important but what it can provide in the way of nutrition. Some ingredients are preferred more than others by the hen.

The following nutrients are present in the ingredients we use to feed poultry at varying levels:

- Carbohydrates

  o An essential energy source

- Protein (amino acids)

  o Protein provides amino acids essential for growth and repair. Fed in excess, protein can be converted into an energy source but it's an expensive option.

- Fats & Oils

  o A concentrated energy source and extremely import in the layer hen diet

- Mineral

  o Essential in many regulating many body processes and for growth and repair

- Vitamins

  o Also used to regulate body processes. Most vitamins can only be supplied in the diet

It is rare to have a single ingredient diet for layer hens. Ingredients differ on the basis of how much they can be included in the diet and what nutrients they supply or what anti-nutritional factors they contain.

Maximizing and Maintaining Egg Lay Rate

From approximately 18 to 22 weeks of age, hens enter their laying period and will reach a peak of lay at around 32 weeks of age. The hens also continue to grow and develop during this time and there is a steady increase in feed intake from 80 to 110 grams of feed per day (The Poultry Hub, 2014).

The objective of layer nutrition is efficient egg production by providing appropriate diets that will maintain the birds in good health and body condition as economically as possible. Different layer breeders recommend different feeding approaches for their hens, including phase feeding or a number of different diets fed during the laying stage that reflect the different ages of the birds. Feed intake can be affected by the level of energy in the diet, the breed of hen, the stage of production, and environmental temperature.

To a large extent, the long term productivity of the layer hen is dependent upon the diet fed during the initial growth stage, before onset of lay. Birds may mature at lighter weights impacting on the lifetime egg production unless the producer is able to feed the bird to bring body weight up to normal in the early lay stage (Leeson & Summers, 2012).

For economic reasons and for the production of the desired egg qualities, phase feeding is often introduced to adjust the protein and amino acid level of the bird's diet as the hens progress through the laying cycle.

The hens' feed intake is driven by a few different factors, including, rate of egg lay, egg weight, body weight and age, ambient temperature, nutrient imbalances, and energy content. Energy content is especially important because the hen will increase or decrease feed intake to maintain energy consumption within a given range. What this means is that the hen will attempt to eat more of a low energy diet than of a high energy diet. Accurate records of true feed intake are crucial to formulate effective diets because the hens' feed consumption will vary with age, environmental temperature and dietary energy content (Hyline, 2014).

Energy

Energy is required by the laying hen for growth and reproduction and is supplied by carbohydrates, fats and oils and protein.

44

Laying hens regulate their feed intake according to their energy requirement when fed ad libitum. The requirement is then determined by the body weight (maintenance), the growth rate, the production level, and the ambient temperature.

The hen's peak energy needs are at about 35 weeks of age, however there is no evidence that the energy level in the diet needs to be adjusted as the birds progress through the laying cycle. The layer hen can adjust its intake quite precisely according to its energy needs by a change in feed intake (Leeson & Summers, 2012).

Egg production records are the best indicator of adequate dietary energy as energy consumption is the most important nutritional factor determining the rate of egg production (Leeson, 2009).

Protein and Amino Acids
Laying hens do not require protein as such, they need the amino acids that make up protein. There is also a change in the hen's requirement for individual amino acids due to genetics, age or environmental factors.

Perez-Bonilla, et al.(2012) concluded that brown laying hens do not need more than 16.5 % crude protein to maximise egg production, as long as the diet meets the requirements for key essential amino acids.

Most small farms opt for the one commercially prepared feed of approximately 17% CP because feeding different ratios to each flock can be complicated or expensive without economy of scale.

Lipids (Fats and Oils)
Linoleic acid is essential in the hen's diet and should be maintained constant at 1.15% (Grobas, et al., 1999) although an increase to 2% is often made early in the laying cycle to increase egg size. A reduction in levels of linoleic acid does not correspond to a decrease in egg size in the latter stages of the laying cycle (Leeson & Summers, 2012). While a decrease in levels of linoleic acid will not reduce egg size, an increase after 65 weeks of age will increase yolk size by up to 4% and the yolk to albumen ration by up to 3.7% (Grobas, et al., 1999).

Fats are an excellent source of energy for laying hens however, the optimal level should be 5% of the diet as higher levels may lead to an increase in fat retention.

In a natural setting, hens would consume oil seeds, nuts, plants and carrion that would supply the fats they require in the diet.

Examples of layer diets (at 100 grams per day intake level) (Poultry Hub, 2017)

Nutrients	Units	1-32 wks	32-44 wks	44-55 wks	> 55 wks
Metabolisable Energy	MJ/kg	11.60-11.97	11.41-11.97	11.20-11.97	10.68-11.83
	kcal/kg	2770-2860	2725-2860	2675-2860	2550-2825
Crude protein	%	19.80	17.50	17.00	16.00
Lysine	%	1.02	0.93	0.89	0.83
Methionine	%	0.51	0.46	0.41	0.38
Linoleic acid	%	1.10	1.60	1.60	1.60
Calcium	%	4.40	4.25	4.50	4.75
Av.phosphorous	%	0.48	0.40	0.36	0.35

Vitamins and Minerals

Much of the phosphorus in feed of plant origin e.g. grains, is unavailable and bound by phytate and is not absorbed by the birds. Therefore, it is critical that available phosphorus, and not the total phosphorus levels, be reflected in the feed formulation. Calcium in the diet depends on its ratio to the available phosphorus and the level of calcium in the formulation. For growing poultry, this ratio should be 2:1 (The Merck Veterinary Manual, 2014). The calcium requirement of laying hens is very high and increases as the hen ages and with the rate of egg production (Centraal Veevoederbureau (CVB), 2009). The eggshell contains approximately 2 g calcium regardless of the hen's age. The shell becomes thinner as the hen ages and the egg becomes larger. The bird's ability to absorb calcium from the intestine also diminishes.

Body weight and feed consumption targets (Poultry Hub, 2017)

Age (wk)	Body weight (g)	Feed consumption (g/bird/day)
1	70	13
2	115	20
3	190	25
4	280	29
5	380-390	33
6	480-500	37
7	580-620	41
8	680-750	46
10	870-970	56
11	960-1080	61
12	1050-1117	66
13	1130-1250	70
14	1210-1310	73
15	1290-1370	75
16	1360-1430	77
17	1500-1540	80

Water

Layer hens will drink at least 50% more water when the temperature rises to 35° C compared to consumption at 22° C. As a rise in temperature signals a decrease in feed intake and an increase in the consumption of water, there is an opportunity to provide limiting nutrients in the water supply. Hens also respond well to cooled water which can result in an increase in feed intake by around 10% (Leeson & Summers, 2012).

Typical daily water consumption for layers (Poultry Hub, 2017)

Production Stage	Age/Rate of Production	Litres of water per 1000 birds at 21°C
Layer pullet	4 weeks	100
	12 weeks	160
	18 weeks	200
Laying hens	50% production	220
	90% production	270

Source: Poultry CRC

Phase Feeding

Phase feeding is the reduction in the protein and amino acid level of the bird's diet as the hens progress through the laying cycle. Feed intake and egg size increase as the hens get older but egg production decreases. It is therefore more economical to reduce the nutrient content of the feed and by doing so, reduce egg size and feed costs. Table 2 indicates the level of major nutrients required at different stages of egg production and appropriate diets for each phase (The Poultry Hub, 2014).

When phase feeding requires that feed be restricted during the laying period, it should not occur until after the maximum egg mass production has been clearly passed (approximately 45-50 weeks). A good rule of thumb is that for each gram of egg mass less laid, provide one gram less of feed (Centraal Veevoederbureau (CVB), 2009).

Phase feeding in a smaller operation may not make much difference to the bottom line and is usually only practiced in very large operations.

Unless you grow your own grain or you are a large egg business, it is often uneconomical to mill and mix your own feed. As you now know, nutrition for layer hens can be quite complex so letting a feed company take care of that for you usually gives you the best outcome. These feed mills will also understand your production system and advise the correct feed for your farm.

Effects of Heat (ambient temperature) on nutritional requirements during the laying cycle

High temperatures cause food intake to decline resulting in inadequate feed consumption and poor performance. When feed intake is reduced because of high environmental temperatures egg output is adversely effected but changes in feed formulation by adjusting the nutrient density can help alleviate the problem along with management of the housing and cooling systems.

Care must be taken when considering any changes to the diet and forward planning based on weather predictions should be implemented as abrupt change can result in further stress for the birds. Leeson & Summers (2012) suggest that when temperatures rise to 36 – 40° that no immediate changes be made as this could result in death.

Changes in egg quality, mass and weight throughout the laying cycle

Albumen and yolk weights increase with the age of the hen with most of the increase being in the weight of the yolk. Shell weight also increases with age but not at the same rate as that of the egg weight. The ratio of yolk to egg white increases with the age of the hens.

Egg shell quality is also affected by the age of the hen as it consists mainly of calcium carbonate (C_aCO_3). Shell quality declines as the hen ages mainly because as egg weight increases, there is no proportionate increase in shell deposition. This effectively means that there is still only the same amount of shell produced but it has to stretch over a larger area making it thinner. Dysfunction of the shell gland may also contribute to the decline in shell quality. In order to improve shell egg quality in the latter stages of the laying cycle, calcium levels in the diet must be increased as the birds get older (Leeson & Summers, 2012).

Feeding management for layer pullets is critical to the lifetime productivity of the birds and the profitability of the farm enterprise. Pullets that enter the laying period when underweight will not perform as well unless they can be fed enough to bring them up to acceptable weight quite quickly. All birds are still growing at the beginning of the laying cycle and their nutrition needs to be managed for optimal egg production but also to maintain acceptable growth rates. If the birds do not reach sexual maturity at the desired age there is a risk of obesity and decreased lifetime egg production.

As the hen ages her nutritional requirements change, as does the size and mass of the egg and the quality of the shell itself. As the hen matures her need for calcium also increases. The bird's diet is then managed to meet those requirements but also to reduce feed costs and improve egg quality and size as the hen moves through the laying cycle.

Free Choice Feeding

Owners of smaller flocks might find this option attractive. The hens are provided with separate feeders for grain and supplements and they are allowed to choose how much of each they want to eat.

Bennett (2003), found that free choice fed hens will lay as many eggs as hens fed a layer hen ration as long as some basic rules are followed:

- Don't give too many choices to the hens. Three choices will work the best and they should be grain, supplement and limestone (or oyster shell). If you are using more than one type of grain, they should be mixed together.
- These choices should be nutritionally distinct; grains high in energy, supplement high in protein and vitamins and limestone high in calcium.
- Introduce the birds to a free choice system 4 weeks before the onset of lay (around 14 weeks of age), this will give the hens time to learn how to feed themselves before the nutritional demands of egg production. It also gives the pullets time to increase their calcium intake and to build reserves in their bones. The gizzard will also need time to adapt and build muscle mass to grind whole grains. This will take about three weeks.
- Vitamins or micro minerals should not be provided in a separate container. Mix these into the supplement because the hens may dislike the taste and not consume enough or over eat and suffer toxic side effects.
- Give the birds adequate feeder space and provide several feeders for each feed type.

Your birds can successfully consume approximately 70% of their diet as whole grain because they are well equipped with a powerful gizzard to do so. The gizzard is a muscle that uses a grinding action to break down the grains with the aid of grit and small pebbles that the hen consumes in its environment. This is why it is so important for hens to have access to shell grit or course soils.

If you look at the composition of an egg and what nutrients each of the three parts contain (see The Eggs), it will make perfect sense why choice feeding is broken down to the three food sources, energy, protein and minerals. The protein supplement will usually contain oil seeds or grains that will supply adequate levels of fats.

Whole grains can yield more metabolizable energy than ground or pelleted grains because of increased efficiency of feed utilisation (Henuk & Dingle, 2002). It should be noted that hens do have a more difficult time eating whole corn (maize). Choice fed hens can lay heavier eggs and consume less food than those fed complete diets. Hens have the ability to learn to selectively consume calcium to meet maintenance and production requirements in response to need (Hughes & Wood-Gush, 1971). This can result in a reduced cost of production per egg.

Egg mass improves because of the increase in calcium consumption that produces a thicker egg shell. It was also found that free choice fed hens produced eggs with darker yolk colour (Olver & Malan, 2000).

A big plus for free choice feeding is that it will develop an active functioning gizzard and this can play a role in the hen's resistance to coccidiosis (Cummings, 1992b).

Free choice feeding is a much more natural approach to feeding layer hens that allows them the freedom to indulge their appetites, develop a robust intestinal tract and resistance to disease, after all, it is what they would be doing in a primal environment.

Pasture as a food source

It's an idyllic picture, hens roaming freely and grazing green pastures. The fact is that your productive hens cannot live on pasture alone. We have already outlined the dietary needs of layer hens so this should make perfect sense now. Pastures will not provide the balance of energy and protein that the birds need to be able to produce the number of eggs needed to keep you in business.

Not all pastures are the same either. Long, dry grasses have little nutritional value and can cause problems for the hens. Different species of grass vary in their nutritional makeup tremendously and if you want pasture to play a real part in your birds diet, you will need to identify the grasses and research their value.

Well managed pastures will provide some nutrition for the birds but just how much will depend on the species of fodder or grass, the growing season, maintenance of the pasture (mowing) and availability of irrigation. A good pasture for grazing hens consists of perennial ryegrass and clover which could yield 15 tonne of dry matter per hectare per year. Pastures should be grazed in the middle phase of its growth cycle because if it is grazed too early recovery will be slow while if left too late, a lower quality pasture will result. Poultry do not make efficient use of long pasture.

In a study by Golden, Arbona, & Anderson (2012) it was found that grazing available to free-range hens on pasture did not provide hens with high enough protein levels, and was not of a composition necessary to support the same level of production as caged hens that were being fed a concentrated and balanced diet so productivity could be slightly lower than caged birds.

It is possible to provide up to 20% of the birds nutritional needs from pasture but it is recommended to have feed available to the birds at all times and to formulate the correct diet as pasture consumption will vary between individual hens. As a guide, Crude Protein should be approximately 17% (although the levels of amino acid are of more concern) and although the birds may source considerable amounts of calcium from the soils, shell grit should still be supplied to assist the gizzard's grinding action, to enable the hen to better cope with fibrous grasses and to store reserves of calcium in older hens. Hens should be fed a mash feed rather than pellets.

Below are pictures of dissected gizzards from pastured chickens. It is clearly evident how much pasture grazing birds will consume. The first picture shows the amount of small pebbles contained inside the gizzard of a mature bird that were used to grind the feed and grasses. When an inadequate diet is offered to hens, they may over consume pasture in an attempt to compensate for the nutritional deficit.

If your hens do not have access to gravelly soil or course shell grit, undigested pasture can become compacted in the gizzard and the bird will probably die.

The next picture shows the major muscles of the gizzard and how they would work together with pebbles and grit to grind feed in young birds. Note how much larger the gizzard is of the older hen.

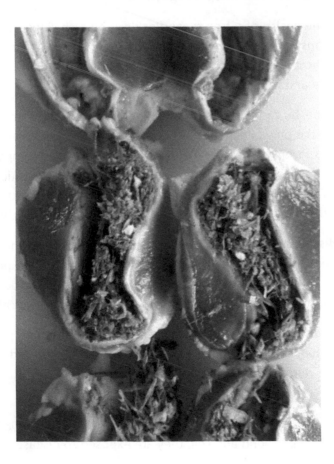

Disease Management

Know what is normal in your flock will help you quickly recognise when something is abnormal so here are some signs that you should be aware of or be monitoring:

- Amount of feed and water consumed
- The normal appearance of droppings
- Egg lay rate
- Growth rate (pullets)
- General appearance of the birds. Look for ruffle feathers, closed eye lids, drooping wings etc.
- Look for watery droppings

If hens start to die, don't wait until things get out of hand. Have a carcass tested by your vet or department of agriculture.

Maintaining the health of a free range flock can be a challenge and requires good stockmanship, a robust vaccination program, good hygiene practices and a mobile housing system that permits the management of contamination risks in pasture and paddock rotations.

Viruses are the biggest infectious disease threat to poultry and therefore vaccination is the only effective tool to control an outbreak. Disease of most importance to layer hens are Marek's Disease, Infectious Laryngotracheitis, Newcastle Disease, Fowl Cholera, Infectious Coryza, Necrotic Enteritis, Coccidiosis, E. coli and Infectious Bronchitis. Diseases of poultry can be divided into three main categories: Behavioural, Metabolic and Infectious.

Metabolic diseases occur when the nutrition of the birds is not balanced and either does not meet, or exceeds their needs. Weak bones and poor quality egg shell and Fatty Liver Disease are just two problems that can be prevented by following diet advice provided by the breeder of the chosen strain.

Behavioural disease is most commonly exhibited as feather pecking and cannibalism that can be managed by avoiding, addressing and preventing stress in the birds or behavioural changes that can result in pecking behaviour.

Infectious causes may be viral or bacterial and because free range birds are in contact with the ground and soil, they are exposed to disease and internal parasites through faecal oral cycling. Control of those diseases that cannot be vaccinated against can be expensive and difficult and management of the environment is critical.

Parasitic disease includes roundworms, tapeworms, fluke, lice, mites, ticks, flies and fleas but the parasite of most significance is coccidiosis. Parasitic disease requires contact with an intermediate host such as wild birds and animals and insects or poor biosecurity and transfer via staff and equipment.

Of the infectious diseases, vaccines are available for the following:

- Marek's disease
- Newcastle disease
- Avian hepatitis
- Infectious bronchitis
- E. coli
- Salmonella
- Bursal disease virus
- Infectious laryngotracheitis
- Erysipelas
- Coryza
- Fowl pox
- Fowl cholera

As free range meat and egg production becomes more popular it can present issues that will not be confronted by the intensive indoor producers. Free range now fits into two categories because of the vast differences in the production systems: Intensive free range (spend most of the time in sheds at high stocking rates) and Pastured Free Range (low stocking rates, small flock sizes).

Inadequate nutrition can cause birds to over consume lush, long pastures resulting in the crop and gizzard becoming impacted with fibrous material especially in Pastured Free Range systems.

Vaccinations

Should your flock be vaccinated? Absolutely they should! All incubated chicks must be vaccinated especially if you operating a commercial enterprise. Here is why.

Humans receive passive immunity from their mother via the placenta before they are born so we come into this world with some protection from disease. Livestock such as cattle, pigs and sheep are not born with this same immunity, they must get it from colostrum (first milk) in the first few hours of life and this will give them some protection for the first few weeks while they are suckling on their mothers and acquiring their own natural immunity from exposure to their environment.

Although chickens are hatched from an egg, they still receive antibodies (passive immunity) to diseases that the mother hen was exposed to or vaccinated against via that egg. This immunity however is very short lived but generally protects the newly hatched chick for the first few days of life while the chicken develops its own immune system.

Now, let's go back to nature for a moment. Think about chicks that have been hatched under a hen, in a nest that would probably be contaminated with all sorts of pathogens from the hen's environment and the hen herself. The chicks hatch and are brooded under the wings and feathers of the hen and generally stay in that nest for a day or two and often return at night. Within 24 hours of all chicks hatching, the hen could have them out pecking around! In a natural setting these chicks are being exposed to diseases in their environment while under the protection of the passive immunity they received while in the egg.   While they are protected, they have the opportunity to build their own acquired immunity to those diseases.

What happens when a chick is hatched in a sterile environment like a commercial hatchery?

There is little opportunity for a hatchery chick to build its immune system and then within days it is transported to a totally new environment, one that could have diseases that its mother had never been exposed to or vaccinated against. Passive immunity is short lived so it has gone, leaving these chicks extremely vulnerable to disease.

It is important that you protect your birds from disease because not only will sickness effect the hens' productivity, some diseases are capable of wiping out your entire flock and impacting on other egg businesses. One of the advantages of buying point of lay pullets is that they can arrive on farm fully vaccinated with little need for you to have to carry out any more treatment as long as you have good farm biosecurity, look after the nutritional requirements of the birds and monitor and manage bird health.

Biosecurity

Pastured production comes with many responsibilities that include animal welfare, food safety and environmental stewardship, but the issue of biosecurity is often misunderstood or ignored. Biosecurity is not just about protecting your flock from disease, it helps to keep our country free of exotic diseases.

Biosecurity plays a crucial role in the prevention of disease on a pastured egg farm which essentially means restricting movement of birds and people on the farm. Avian influenza can be spread by wild waterfowl so when surface water is used to supply the birds it must be sanitized. Poultry farms and range areas should be established away from water sources such as dams to minimize the risk of contact with wild birds by the hens. Biosecurity at a practical level is about designing a plan to minimize the introduction of disease from any source.

You will find more information on Biosecurity for Australian flocks in the Standards section but here are some simple guidelines for keeping you flock healthy:

- Buy birds from a reputable source
- Quarantine all new birds
- Never mix birds of different species
- Do not mix birds of different ages
- Inspect birds regular and investigate anything different
- Keep housing and paddocks clean
- Store feed so that it is rodent and bird proof
- Do not let visitors roam freely amongst your birds
- Supply visitors with footbath or boots and overalls
- Report any suspect disease in your flock

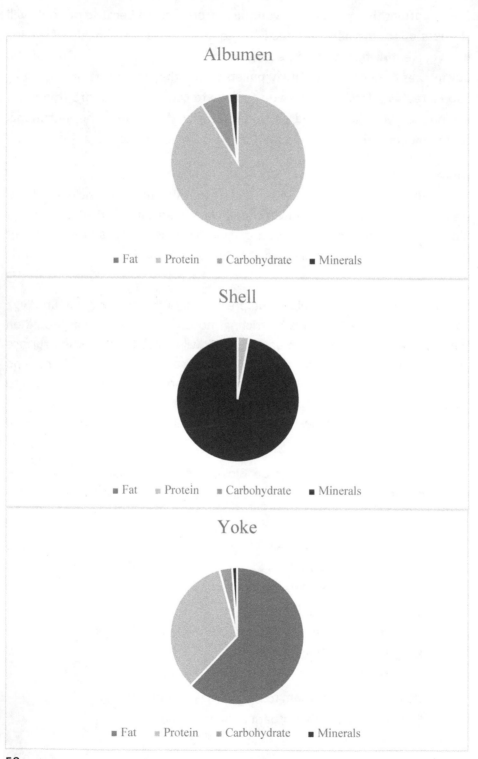

CHICKEN EGG

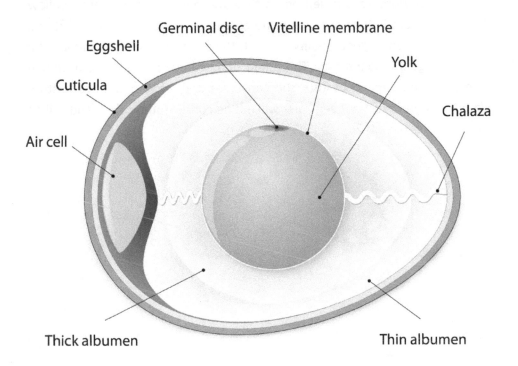

There are three very distinct parts of the egg; the yoke, the white (albumen) and the shell and when you examine to composition of these parts, it is easier to understand the role good nutrition plays in producing the best eggs. It is also evident why one feed ingredient alone cannot supply all the needed nutrients to produce these eggs.

Yolk Colour

There is an incorrect assumption that the colour of the egg yolk will distinguish a pastured or free range egg from one that is intensively reared. This is incorrect. A uniform depth of colour (particularly very dark, deep orange) is more of an indicator that yolk colouring agents have been added to the hens feed.

If an intensively produced egg, a caged egg for example, was produced from a hen that did not have a colouring agent added to its feed the yolk would be an extremely pale, lemon colour.

Yolks in eggs from hens raised on pasture are much brighter orange/yellow than those from indoor hens when no colouring agents have been fed and pasture has been of good quality. In fact, the colour is sometimes more of a fluoro orange it is so intense. The colour of pastured eggs will vary from hen to hen and how much pasture she consumes and what species of pasture plant she prefers so, your egg yolks will not be consistent in colour and will be varied shades of yellow.

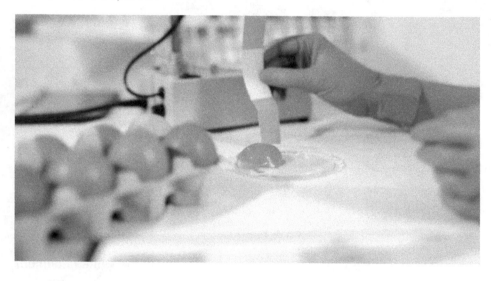

How does green grass make the yolks yellow?

Many plants contain yellow pigments called xanthophyll. Xanthophylls means yellow leaves. Natural sources of these carotenoid pigments can be found in carrots (not very strong), chilli, corn, marigolds, lucerne and algae as well as good old grass.

To get that deep, dark orange yolk that you often see in caged eggs, it is necessary to add a red colouring to the feed as well as the yellow. Industry does not always use natural colouring options. Many of the colouring agents are synthetic.

It may be necessary even for pastured egg producers to add colouring to their feed at times especially in summer when there may not be much green feed available. There is a misconception that the yellower the egg is the more likely it is to be from a free range hen and that pale yolk are from unhealthy birds. Consumers will come to understand the difference in time.

Pale yolks can be an indicator of disease because poor health can reduce pigment absorption. If your hens have plenty of green feed but their yolks are getting pale, suspect disease.

Collecting and Cleaning Eggs

As we discussed earlier, egg collection systems vary from automated roll away systems to simple nest boxes than require the eggs to be picked up by hand. It will depend on the surrounding environment, the number of nest boxes, training of the birds and the conditions within the laying area on how dirty your eggs are going to get and how much cleaning needs to be done.

Under the Australian Food Standards Code 4.2.5 an egg producer must not sell or supply eggs or egg pulp for human consumption if the eggs are unacceptable.

An unacceptable egg is:

a. a cracked egg or a dirty egg, or
b. egg product which has not been processed in accordance with the Standard, or
c. egg product which contains a pathogenic micro-organism, whether or not the egg product has been processed in accordance with the Standard.

Egg businesses that produce and wash or clean and grade eggs for human consumption must implement appropriate cleaning procedures to ensure the safety of their product.

Dirty eggs can be a health hazard if they are not handled correctly. Dirty eggs can carry harmful bacteria that can enter the eggs and if not cooked properly they can potentially cause food poisoning.

Dirty eggs must not be sold for retail sale. Dirty eggs must be either:

a. cleaned so that visible faeces, soil and other matter is removed from the shell, or

b. sold to a licensed egg business that washes or dry cleans, or

c. discarded.

Eggs should be collected often, at least once per day, to help decrease the number of dirty and cracked eggs.

Collection of eggs should be more frequent during very hot and cold weather.

Important points to remember when collecting eggs:

- clean eggs should be separated from dirty eggs
- eggs should be collected in an easy to clean container like coated wire baskets or plastic flats. This will prevent stains from rusted metal and contamination from other materials which are difficult to clean and sanitise
- do not stack eggs too high. If collecting in baskets do not stack eggs more than 5 layers deep. If using plastic flats do not stack more than 6 flats
- eggs should be held below 15°C with 70% humidity prior to cleaning
- embryos can start to develop in fertile eggs held at a temperature of 29°C for more than a few hours
- never cool eggs rapidly before cleaning. The egg shell will contract and may pull any dirt or bacteria on the egg surface into the pores when cooled
- keep egg temperature fairly constant until the eggs are washed to avoid sweating
- sweating occurs when eggs are moved from cold storage to a warm environment, and
- condensation on the surface of the egg facilitates movement of microbes inside the shell.

Source: (NSW Food Authority, 2017)

Dry cleaning eggs

The following information on cleaning and washing eggs is an excerpt from the NSW Food Authority guidelines to comply with the Egg Food Safety Scheme of Food Regulation 2015 (NSW Food Authority, 2017).

Eggs that are only slightly dirty can be cleaned or rubbed with an egg brush, paper towel, sanding sponge or plastic scourer with a gentle rubbing action. Dirty eggs with mud or faeces that cannot be removed easily using this method should be separated for clean eggs and/or disposed of.

- If a dry cloth is used it must be changed if there is any sign of soiling and there should be enough cloths to ensure that only a clean cloth is passed over the egg each time
- Dirty cloths must be sanitized, washed and dried thoroughly before reuse
- Any cloth or material used to dry clean eggs must be food safe
- Disposable paper towels avoid re-use so are highly recommended

Precautions must be taken if using a damp cloth to clean eggs:

- Wash water must be sanitized and changed often
- Sanitizers and detergents must be food safe and only used as per the manufacturer's instructions
- Damp cloths should not be dripping wet. They should be rinsed in sanitized water and thoroughly wrung out.
- No water should be left on the egg surface. A fine film of moisture that is readily evaporated should only be seen

All cleaning equipment should be sanitised in 100 ppm of chlorine for 20 minutes. Sanding blocks should not be used as they are not food grade.

Egg Washing

A lot of care needs to be taken when washing eggs because egg shells are very porous and washing can allow microorganisms to enter through the shell. Eggs will contract as they cool down and this may cause wash water to enter the egg.

- Minimize the chance of deterioration of quality and contamination from other eggs by washing as soon as eggs are collected
- Wash water should be held at a temperature of 41 – 44 $^\circ$ C

- The washing process should not allow the eggs to stand or soak in the wash water
- Eggs should be dried after washing or the risk of contamination is increased

There is a lot more information available from the Food Authority on their website. Look for the equivalent in your state.

http://www.foodauthority.nsw.gov.au/_Documents/industry/egg_cleaning_p rocedures.pdf

Candling Eggs

Eggs should be candled (or passed over a light) to find any fine cracks or internal problems with the egg. e.g. bloodspots. Candlers can be simple home made units consisting of a light source that is confined to a narrow area using pvc pipe, a timber box etc., right through to purpose built benchtop units or integrated candler/grader combinations. Have a look on YouTube for ideas.

Blood spots

Blood spots are harmless but unfortunately, they can be a real turn off for the consumer who often believes that it is a fertilised egg so it is a good idea to remove them from sale during the candling process. Bloodspots are caused by a rupture of a blood vessel on the yolk surface during the formation of the egg. The cause may be the breed of bird, bullying and fighting, too much lucerne in the diet (interferes with vitamin K), fungal toxins or sometimes disease. If you suddenly get a lot of eggs with blood spots it should be investigated.

Grading Eggs

As a small producer, you may get away with not sorting your eggs by weight, but, most retailers will want their eggs sorted by traditional weight categories (e.g. 600, 700 or 800 grams), and packaged and labelled accordingly.

Egg Stamping

It is now a requirement to stamp eggs that are offered for sale. Each state may have some variance or allowance for very small producers so check with your state food safety authority.

The requirements are:

(1) An egg processor must not sell eggs unless each individual egg is marked with the processor's or producer's unique identification.

(2) An egg processor must not sell or supply egg product unless each package or container containing the egg product is marked with the processor's or producer's unique identification.

Egg Packaging

In Australia there are legal requirements for how you label and package your eggs. Businesses that produce eggs must implement measures to control food safety hazards and must be able to trace their individual eggs for sale as well as demonstrate compliance with Australia New Zealand Food Standards Code - Standard 4.2.5 – Primary Production and Processing Standard for Eggs and Egg Product. The section of this standard covering primary egg production covers:

- General food safety management
- Inputs
- Waste disposal
- Health and hygiene requirements
- Skills and knowledge
- Design, construction and maintenance of premises, equipment and transportation vehicles
- Bird health
- Traceability
- Sale or supply

Division 2 – Primary production of eggs (the following is an extract from the Standard)

3   General food safety management

(1)   An egg producer must systematically examine all of its production operations to identify potential hazards and implement control measures to address those hazards.

(2)   An egg producer must also have evidence to show that a systematic examination has been undertaken and that control measures for those identified hazards have been implemented.

(3) An egg producer must operate according to a food safety management statement that sets out how the requirements of this Division are to be or are being complied with.

4 Inputs

An egg producer must take all reasonable measures to ensure inputs do not make the eggs unsafe or unsuitable.

- Editorial note:
- See the definitions of 'safe' and 'suitable' in Standard 3.1.1.

See the definition of 'inputs' in Standard 4.1.1 which includes feed, water and chemicals used in or in connection with the primary production activity.

5 Waste disposal

(1) An egg producer must store, handle or dispose of waste in a manner that will not make the egg unsafe or unsuitable.

(2) For subclause (1), waste includes sewage, waste water, used litter, dead birds, garbage and eggs which the proprietor, supervisor or employee of the egg producer knows, ought to reasonably know or to reasonably suspect, are unsafe or unsuitable.

6 Health and hygiene requirements

(1) A person involved in egg production must exercise personal hygiene and health practices that do not make the eggs unsafe or unsuitable.

(2) An egg producer must take all reasonable measures to ensure that personnel and visitors exercise personal hygiene and health practices that do not make the eggs unsafe or unsuitable.

7 Skills and knowledge

An egg producer must ensure that a person who engages in or supervises the primary production of eggs has –

(a)   skills in food safety and food hygiene; and

(b)   knowledge of food safety and food hygiene matters; commensurate with their work.

8   **Design, construction and maintenance of premises, equipment and transportation vehicles**

An egg producer must –

(a)   ensure that premises, equipment and transportation vehicles are designed and constructed in a way that minimises the contamination of the eggs, allows for effective cleaning and sanitisation, and minimises the harbourage of pests and vermin; and

(b)   keep premises, equipment and transportation vehicles effectively cleaned, sanitised and in good repair to ensure the eggs are not made unsafe or unsuitable.

9   **Bird health**

(1)   An egg producer must not obtain eggs for human consumption from birds if the proprietor, supervisor or employee of the egg producer knows, ought to reasonably know or to reasonably suspect, the bird is affected by disease or a condition that makes the eggs unsafe or unsuitable.

(2)   The definition of 'condition' in Standard 3.2.2 does not apply to this clause.

10   **Traceability**

(1)   An egg producer must not sell eggs unless each individual egg is marked with the producers' unique identification.

(2)   An egg producer who supplies egg pulp must mark each package or container containing the pulp with the producers' unique identification.

(3)   Subclauses (1) and (2) do not apply to eggs or egg pulp sold or supplied to an egg processor (the supplied product) if that egg processor complies with clause 20 in respect of the supplied product.

(4)   In addition to subclauses (1) and (2), an egg producer must have a system to identify to whom eggs or egg pulp is sold or supplied.

11   Sale or supply

(1)   An egg producer must not sell or supply eggs or egg pulp for human consumption if it knows, ought to reasonably know or to reasonably suspect, that the eggs are unacceptable.

(2)   Subclause (1) does not apply to an egg producer that sells or supplies unacceptable eggs to an egg processor for processing in accordance with clause 21.

(Australian Government Federal Register of Legislation, n.d.)

Egg Carton Labels

Pastured is a term that is rapidly gaining popularity with consumers because it more accurately defines the conditions under which they expect their eggs to be produced. It also enables the producer to set themselves apart from what has now become a supermarket label, 'free range'.

When it comes to eggs, many producers have been led to believe that there is a legal requirement to label their eggs as either caged, barn or free range in line with the model code and this has caused a great deal of despair for those farmers that produce their eggs under such different conditions to the corporate giants that have taken over the term free range. Levelling the playing field will only serve to put small farms out of business and lead consumers down the same old path of deception.

PROOF (Pastured Raised On Open Fields) has been a leader in steering a new direction for both egg and pork producers and is working to ensure that our farmers hold on to their rightful place in the market and in doing so act, on sound advice.

PROOF has sought legal advice on the requirements for labelling on egg cartons and our producers are free to label their eggs as 'pastured' because there is no legal requirement to call them cage, barn or free range only*.

The term pastured eggs would convey the impression that laying hens have reasonable access to and graze on pasture outside. The expression also conveys the impression that the diet of the laying hen substantially or meaningfully comprises of grass pasture (as opposed to exclusively relying on supplied feed stock), particularly if the term free range is used in conjunction with the term pastured. (If the term free range is included on your label you must comply with the new information standard when it comes into force. It will not be necessary for eggs simply labelled as pastured)

On this basis, egg producers who use the term pastured eggs, must allow their laying hens access to grassy pasture to permit the hens to feed on grass in order to avoid contravention of the consumer protection laws.

Our advice also recommends that to further mitigate the risk of contravening consumer law provisions, that more information about the meaning of 'pastured eggs' be provided on the carton by using the PROOF definition for pastured production or using the PROOF logo and website link available to PROOF licensees.

It is very important farmers are able to offer proof that their production system is genuinely pasture based so as not to mislead consumers, but to also ensure that our farmers have secure and viable future. Learn more about PROOF Licensing on the website www.pastured.com.au

While the Australian Egg Corporation has provided guidelines for producers that stipulated that the terms caged, barn or free range be used on egg cartons, this is a voluntary guideline. However, the Egg Corp Assured program does dictate that producers comply with the Egg Corporation guideline. So, the only restrictions on how production systems are described on egg cartons are if the producers are Egg Corp Assured or in the ACT.

*except in the ACT

Food Safety

A range of microbiological hazards may be introduced into poultry during the primary production phase. These include bacterial pathogens introduced through contaminated feed, water and the environment.

Salmonella

The Australian poultry industry is considered to be free from Salmonella enteritidis although it is a most important to the food industry worldwide. However, Salmonella typhimurium has been isolated from layer farms in Australia and Salmonella infantisis the predominant pathogen in the Australian egg industry.

Infected chickens transmit Salmonella to eggs especially when their environment is contaminated by carriers such as rats, mice, birds and flies. A hen will show no outward signs of illness once infected, but small deposits of salmonella may be found in her eggs. Small amounts of salmonella may be relatively harmless but it can increase rapidly to dangerous levels if the eggs aren't cooled quick enough and kept at the right temperature during storage and shipment. Eggs can also be infected with salmonella from the outside by coming into contact with the bacteria in a contaminated environment or on dirty equipment.

Salmonella growth in an egg occurs after the membrane surrounding the egg yolk breaks down. This takes a considerable period of time but is more rapid at warm temperatures. Concentration of aerobic bacteria, E. coli, yeasts and moulds on the eggs shell can be significantly reduce during commercial egg washing. Refrigeration has been identified as one the most critical issues in minimizing the risks associated with Salmonella contamination in eggs and they should be stored as low 4°C as rapid growth of salmonella will occur at 25°C. Managing temperature is a critical step in preventing high levels of contamination in eggs.

There have been many changes in egg production systems as well as the egg itself. Free range production will contribute to the microbial challenges the industry faces if good management is not in place.

Salmonella is the principal microorganism of human health concern associated with eggs and egg products. The frequency of Salmonella-contaminated eggs in Australia is very low but there is a potential risk of illness from consumption of raw or lightly-cooked eggs, or the consumption of uncooked foods containing raw egg.

Remember: It is illegal to re-use egg cartons

Pasture Management

Raising chickens on pasture is not a new idea, history has shown us that for centuries hens were kept in a more natural environment that included foraging in forests and grasslands. Intensively housed and fed livestock have only recently become the new normal.

There are a couple of different reasons that people choose to raise hens on pasture and they include wanting to feed birds as naturally as possible to produce the most wholesome and tasty eggs, concerns for bird welfare or simply meeting consumer demand and expectations. This means that pasture will play a different role for different free range systems. In some systems pasture consumption will simply be incidental or it may form a meaningful part of the hen's diet. However, no matter what part pasture will play in how your hens are fed, you will have to consider the effects the birds will have on the pasture and environment.

When pasture is used as part of a complete, balanced diet it can provide a substantial contribution to the nutritional needs of your flock however, because of the high fibre content and lower energy available in the pasture, a balanced feed ration should also be provided at all times.

How your hens perform on pasture is directly related to the quantity and quality of grass available. You will need to identify the grasses that are in your pasture or have knowledge of the nutritional value of the forage crops you plant. What is critical for all grazed species is how digestible the grass is as this will influence how much the hen will eat, how much nutrient is in the feed and how much of it can actually be digested.

Dry matter in pasture is measured by the amount of water in the grasses. pasture is weighed while wet, then dried and weighed again to work o percentage of dry matter. For example, a good quality, young pasture may be 85% water. This means that while it may appear that the hen is eating an awful lot of grass, a large percentage of it will be water therefore the birds needs to consume a lot of it to get the needed nutrition. Digestibility is a measure of how much of the feed that is eaten is used. If the hen consumes 10 grams of dry matter and then 3 grams of it is excreted then 7 grams, or 70% of it, has been digested. Digestibility is also influenced by the quality of the grass and its stage of growth as this will impact on how fast it is processed by the birds. Young soft shoots and green leafy plants are much more digestible that mature, dry stems. Actively growing grasses will be of much greater nutritional value.

Pastures need to be managed to get the most out of grazing. Paddock rotations, resting pastures, not overgrazing, mowing or slashing and ensuring manure is evenly spread across a paddock will help maintain the grasses and the soil.

Having chickens run outdoors can sometimes pose a risk to the environment if sustainable farming practices are not understood and put into practice.

While we like to refer to the grazing of hens on pasture, we must remember that poultry are not ruminants and cannot get most of their nutritional needs from pasture alone if we are to produce quality eggs. Therefore we need to import or buy in feed to meet the hen's requirements and that means that we will also be adding some of that imported nutrient into the soil deposited there through the hen's manure. When you consider how many birds are in the flock and how much each eats per day, there is the potential for a lot of nutrient to go into the ground. Hens also scratch around and form dust baths and this behaviour can damage plant root systems and bare out extensive areas.

Nutrient loading in the soils can contribute to contamination of water ways and ground waters and is a major concern for regulators. The accumulation of manure in paddocks can cause odour problems for neighbours and encourage the breeding of flies. Unfortunately, the finger has been pointed small producers and authorities have begun giving pastured farmers a hard time when it comes to development applications or neighbour complaints. You must take environmental management of your flock seriously.

Grazing hens on pasture that has grown well because of manure inputs is not going to remove the amount of nutrients needed to bring soil levels down sufficiently. You will have to find another way to take the nutrient out of the soil. You can do this by growing hay and cutting it, simply mowing a paddock and removing what has been cut, growing a crop that is harvested and removed from the land. This is called 'cut and cart' and simply means growing something that will take up the nutrient in the soil and then harvesting it (cut) and removing it from the farm (cart). Resting the paddock will do nothing to remove nutrient from the soil. Allowing extensive rest periods between paddock rotations does mean however that it will take quite some time for nutrient levels to build up, especially if cattle or sheep are allowed to graze the same area.

Keeping good ground cover is also very important to prevent issues with erosion, dust and odour and a good practice is to maintain paddocks at 70% groundcover. You may have to adjust your stocking rates to achieve this.

Managing the even spread of manure across the paddock is important and an effective way to prevent nutrient overloading in concentrated areas. This is easy to achieve when you have a mobile system that allows you to relocate sheds, feeders and watering points throughout the paddock and different locations of the farm. With a systematic approach, manure can be evenly spread through the strategic placement of infrastructure. Make it part of your daily or weekly management plan to move the sheds or caravans (only needs to be a short distance), the feeders and the water. Separating the water and feed supply will ensure that the birds travel back and forth so use this to your advantage. With a little thought and planning you can fertilize an entire paddock with no accumulating of nutrients in confined areas.

Consider the slope of the land in the design of your farm. Very flat land will prevent run off and paddocks may become waterlogged. Steeper slopes are going to allow run off of manure nutrients in heavy rain events that could contaminate dams and waterways as well as cause erosion. Ideally, your lar should not slope more than 10 degrees and more slope will req management strategies such as earth bunding or contour banks to slow the passage of water and nutrient through the property. Development applications are more complicated on hilly land and more unlikely to be approved so careful site selection will save you a lot of trouble. I have found many useful videos on YouTube that explain simple methods of measuring the slope of land.

Getting Down to Business

The cost of producing an egg will vary for each farm due to location and the cost of feed. In will vary dramatically when sound management systems are not in place. Have you heard the saying 'hens pay everyday'? I think by now you will know that this is not necessarily true and to make money from pastured eggs you are going to have to be a good manager, one that is in tune with the flock.

Record Keeping

It's a job most people hate but if you don't do it, how will you know if you are maximising production and profitability? You can't rely on a static number of eggs to be produced each day over the entire lay cycle of the hens. Apart from being unrealistic, there are so many things that can cause disruptions to the rate at which hens lay and the quality of those eggs. For example, to base your numbers on an 80% lay rate you will have to have extremely well bred and raised, vaccinated pullets maintained in a disease and stress free environment with an optimal diet. Then, you will have to replace those birds at the end of their lay cycle and have another flock of pullets ready to take their place. Understand the variations in lay rate by keeping good records and knowing what your true average is. Here are some key records that should be kept:

- **Feed consumption.** How much are the birds eating each day? You can't work out what it costs to produce an egg if you do not know this. Remember that a drop in feed consumption can also translate to a drop in egg production. What is causing then hens to be off their feed?
- **Lay rate**. How many eggs are being produced each day? Divide this number by the number of hens in the flock.
- **Egg quality and size.** Within each flock, eggs should be fairly uniform. Egg size increases with age. Variations in size, colour, texture and

shell quality can all be signs that something is wrong. Review your diet, check over the environment and hen behaviour and be aware that some diseases such Infectious Bronchitis can cause abnormalities in the eggs shell.

- **Mortality rates.** Keep records of every dead bird. Not only will this alert you to health or behavioural problems, you will need to adjust your flock numbers to calculate your lay rate. Allow for at least 5% mortality rate.
- **Packing rate.** How many eggs end up in the carton for sale? Consider the cracked, dirty or distorted eggs that will not be sold. 90% would be a rough guideline. So is that 90% of the lay rate you are basing your profits on?

Lay Rate

Are you aware that it takes approximately 25 hours for an egg to develop in the hen? Expecting an egg every single day is just not possible unless you have a genetically superior bird that is guaranteed to do so. Young birds will lay well in the early stages of the lay cycle and it would be reasonable to expect a 90% lay rate, but, as the lay cycle extends production will drop and could go as low as 50%.

The overall lay rate of 75% for the lay cycle would be reasonable to assume.

These lay rates will only happen when conditions are optimal and every care is taken with disease management, nutrition, environmental management and the birds are kept as stress free as possible. Simple problems can result in a drop in the lay rate: an eagle or hawk takes up residence nearby, sudden fright, extremes in weather conditions just to name a few.

Income and Expenditure

Setup costs for a pastured egg farm will include:

Range area and housing

- Perimeter and internal fencing
- Housing/shelters
- Brooder (if raising chicks)
- Feeders and waterers
- Water tanks
- Water supply (piped to paddocks)

- Irrigation for pasture (if available)
- Machinery to manage pasture and housing relocation (e.g. a small tractor)

Egg Processing

- Egg packing room
- Cool room/fridge
- Egg grader (for larger operations)
- Delivery vehicle

Feed

- Storage silos
- Scales
- Feed mixer/mill (if mixing your own)

Income:

- Eggs
- Sale of spent hens
- Hay/crops

Gross Income:

Annual Variable Costs

- Feed costs
- Pullet replacement costs
- Cartons and outers
- Delivery costs
- Marketing costs
- Medication/Vet
- Electricity
- Repairs and maintenance
- Cost of labour
- Vehicle costs
- Insurance
- Phone
- Accountant
- Legal fees
- Bank interest

- Certification fees
- Stationery
- Travel

Total Costs:

Marketing Your Pastured Eggs

Consumer demand for 'higher welfare' food products has created a market in which egg producers can be rewarded for adhering to welfare standards that are at higher levels than industry minimums such as those set out in the Model Code. The ethical consumer is very interested in how the hen lived its life and that it was afforded a stress free existence while living as close to nature as a controlled farming system will allow.

Transparent farming practices and an honest portrayal of farm activities on social media, advertising and on websites helps to sell the story of the farm and go a long way to offering customers an insight into how the hens live their lives and whether or not their expectations of pastured free range production are being met. Selling your customer the story of your food is vitally important to the acceptance and growth of your brand.

One of the best ways to demonstrate your commitment to hen welfare, sustainable farming and transparency is farm accreditation. This offers the reassurance that someone else is looking over your operation to validate your claims. You will find that, particularly as competition grows, many retailers will ask for, or give preference to, farms that have an accreditation program in place so that they can display this to their customers.

Competition is growing and will continue to do so. Do not get into a price war to sell your product, instead, show your customers why your product is better than your competitor's.

The consumer is interested in sustainable farming and how the flock are integrated into the farm instead of being an isolated part of it. Don't be afraid to talk up your mobile housing, paddock rotations and how you manage pastures or feed grown especially for the hens. Of special interest is the role the birds play in the sustainability of the farm by providing chemical free fertilizer for crops.

The huge demand for free range product and the lack of producers has led to a bit of a scramble to fill the void. Coupled with the lack of a legal defini for what free range means there is some confusion now about the free range labels that are available and standards of production may not be in line with what consumers envisage free range to be.

Farm accreditation schemes play an important role in building consumer confidence in your brand. The welfare standards under which animals are produced are actually a quality characteristic of the eggs you produce and should be recognised as such. Since the welfare of your flock is not self evident to the consumer and has to be taken on trust – choice will be reliant to a major degree on how well your product is labelled and how freely the consumer can access further information about you and the farm.

Key factors in advertising your pastured eggs and building your brand:

- Give a clear picture of what you are offering
- Meet client needs and specifications
- Be unique or have a strong association with consumer needs and wants
- Maintain your position in consumer minds
- Build relationships
- Be Reliable
- Be adaptable and flexible, particularly when starting out
- Sell your story

Building a Brand

Brand is the result of the promises you keep, your passion for pastured chickens and the things you do to let people know about it.

We are in the market to produce food not a raw material. This will be made clear to your customers and potential buyers by transparent farming practice and ensuring that you do practice what you preach.

Focus on doing what you say you will do and keep your promises.

Sell your customer the story of your food. Don't just talk about your passion, make it visible, make your clients feel it too.

Invest in systems that will give returns for the markets you pursue. Is just producing free range eggs enough to keep you ahead of the competition? pastured is more than just keeping hens in a paddock, it encapsulates animal 'fare, sound environmental and farming practices and producing wholesome tasty food. Spend a little time thinking about who you are today – warts and all, and what you need to do to fulfil your promise and improve your operation rather than forging blindly forward with a picture of who you should be and trying to convince someone of a lie.

By showing preferences for 'higher welfare' products, consumers can create a market in which we producers can be rewarded for adhering to welfare standards which are at higher levels than industry minimums.

There is a growing preference for the use of the term 'Pastured' to better define the free range systems we employ because it is better describes hens that are free to roam in open fields or paddocks.

About PROOF – Pasture Raised On Open fields

The PROOF logo is designed to assist consumers in making an informed choice when they purchase pastured free range pork, eggs, meat or chicken. It makes a simple but powerful statement - ask for proof that the free range product you are buying was raised in open paddocks. Our approach to validating the claim of free range is a little different to once a year auditing that is offered by most accreditation bodies. We believe that pastured free range farming is more than just passing an inspection every year to meet a prescribed standard that doesn't necessarily fit with the all farms principles and practices. We keep in touch with farmers throughout the year and our goal is to help them grow and improve where ever possible.

If they wish to participate, our farmers undergo animal welfare and farm management training and on completion validation is provided on our website. Our farmers provide a farm management statement and internal audit that aligns with our Core Values and is their promise that their livestock are genuinely pastured free range. We do not try and fit all our farmers into the one box, instead, we let them show you their level of commitment to animal welfare and sustainable free range farming practices.

Producers

The PROOF logo helps you more clearly identify your pastured free range product. By looking for the distinctive PROOF logo on pastured pork, chicken, meat or egg packaging, the consumer will be able to make a clearer and easier purchasing decision and our policy of transparency means th information about your farm is freely available.

The PROOF logo on packaging is an invitation to learn more about how you farm and to be able to engage in your story through direct links to your website or contact details.

Consumers

Our community of like minded farmers have so much in common and are very proud of what they do. Unfortunately, a lack of a legal definition often sees them struggling to survive against intensively produced, low priced product. When our farmers display the PROOF logo they are inviting you to engage in their story and learn more about their farm so that you know you are making the right choice.

We want to ensure that our farmers fully understand their obligation to the animals they farm as well as complying with regulatory requirements for animal welfare. We do this through training modules and once those modules are completed, they will be displayed along side that farmer's listing. Undergoing training is our way of showing commitment to a sustainable pastured free range operation.

All Licensed farms pledge their commitment to the Core Values of PROOF and our definition of pastured. The Core Values are further expanded in our Guidelines. Our policy of transparency means that all our licensed farms are listed on this website and share their contact and farm details. If you want proof, just ask them.

Standards, Codes of Practice, Human Health and Guidelines (Australia)

Egg Producer License

NSW
Egg producers are businesses or farms that produce more than 20 dozen eggs for sale in any week.

These businesses may also assess eggs for quality (eg. by weight, size) and dry clean dirty eggs.

http://www.foodauthority.nsw.gov.au/industry/eggs/egg-producers

QLD
If you are proposing to undertake primary production or processing activities in relation to eggs you need to apply for accreditation under the Egg and Egg Products Scheme (the Egg Scheme).

http://www.safefood.qld.gov.au/index.php?option=com_content&view=section&id=6&Itemid=32

Vic
Producers with 50 or more egg producing birds

You must have and follow a DEDJTR approved food safety management statement OR be part of an approved industry or commercial quality assurance (QA) program.

http://agriculture.vic.gov.au/agriculture/livestock/poultry-and-eggs/poultry-legislation-regulations-and-standards/food-safety-for-egg-producers/resources-for-egg-producers-with-50-or-more-egg-producing-birds

SA
Egg producers must be accredited if they are involved in any of the following:

- Have more than 50 laying birds.
- Produce and sell eggs to a food business such as a supermarket, café, hotel or bakery.
- Produce and sell eggs to another egg producer.
- Produce and sell eggs at a market (e.g. a farmers' market).

- Produce and sell eggs by wholesale.

Backyard producers who give eggs to friends and family do not need to be accredited.

http://www.pir.sa.gov.au/biosecurity/food_safety/eggs

WA

All poultry and egg producers, whether backyard or commercial, are required to comply with the laws and regulations relevant to their business regardless of the type of production system (organic, free range, barn, cage).

https://www.agric.wa.gov.au/livestock-biosecurity/regulation-poultry-production

Tas

The Egg Food Safety Scheme introduces a mandatory accreditation requirement for commercial egg producers based on the volume of eggs produced.

This production threshold is 20 dozen eggs in any week (and is the equivalent of keeping approximately 50 egg laying birds).

http://dpipwe.tas.gov.au/biosecurity/product-integrity/food-safety/eggs/egg-food-safety-scheme

Egg Processing

Australia New Zealand Food Standards Code - Standard 4.2.5 – Primary Production and Processing Standard for Eggs and Egg Product.

https://www.legislation.gov.au/Details/F2014C00965

http://www.foodauthority.nsw.gov.au/_Documents/industry/egg_cleaning_procedures.pdf

Egg Food Safety Scheme of Food Regulation 2015 (NSW)

http://www.austlii.edu.au/au/legis/nsw/consol_reg/fr2015148/s166.html

you will need to find the equivalent in your state)

Egg Stamping

Australia New Zealand Food Standards Code - Standard 4.2.5 – Primary Production and Processing Standard for Eggs and Egg Product

https://www.legislation.gov.au/Details/F2011L00860

http://www.foodauthority.nsw.gov.au/industry/eggs/egg-stamping

Codes of Practice

Model Code of Practice for the Welfare of Animals – Domestic Poultry

http://www.publish.csiro.au/book/3451

Environmental Guidelines for the Australian Egg Industry

https://www.aecl.org/assets/Uploads/Resources/Environmental-Guidelines-for-the-Australian-Egg-Industry.pdf

Biosecurity

http://www.farmbiosecurity.com.au/

http://farmbiosecurity.com.au/wp-content/uploads/2013/01/National-Farm-Biosecurity-Manual-Poultry-Production.pdf

Publications

Public health and safety of eggs and egg products in Australia

http://www.foodstandards.gov.au/publications/documents/Eggs_healthandsafety.pdf

References

Australian Government Federal Register of Legislation, n.d. *Australia New Zealand Food Standards Code - Standard 4.2.5 – Primary Production and Processing Standard for Eggs and Egg Product.* [Online]
Available at: https://www.legislation.gov.au/Details/F2011L00860
[Accessed Jan 2017].

Bennett, C., 2003. *Choice-feeding of small paying hen flocks,* Winnipeg: Manitoba Agriculture and Food.

Bornstein, S., 1977. *Protein and energy requirements of laying hens and broiler breeders,* Israel: Poultry Science, Agricultural Research Organisation.

Centraal Veevoederbureau (CVB), 2009. *CVB Table Booklet Feeding of Poultry.* Series no. 45 ed. s.l.:CVB.

Coutts , J. A. & Wilson, G. C., 2007. *Optimum Egg Quality - A practical approach.* 1st ed. s.l.:5M Publishing.

Cummings, R. B., 1992b. *The biological control of coccidiosis by choice feeding,* Amsterdam: In Proceedings of XIX Worlds Poultry Congress.

Donkoh, A., 1988. Management of environmental temperature and rations for poultry production in the hot and humid tropics. *International Journal of Bioemteorology,* 32(4), pp. 247-253.

Grobas, S., Mendez, J., De Blas, C. & Mateos, G. G., 1999. Laying Hen Productivity as Affected by Energy, Supplemental Fat, Linoleic Acid Concentration of the Diet. *Poultry Science,* Volume 78, pp. 1542-1551.

Henuk, Y. L. & Dingle, J. G., 2002. Practical and economical advantages of choice feeding systems for laying poultry. *Worlds poultry Science Journal,* Volume 58, pp. 199-208.

Hughes, B. O. & Wood-Gush, D. G., 1971. A specific appetite for clacium in domestic chickens. *Animal Behaviour,* Volume 19, pp. 490-499.

Hyline, 2014. *Feeding the Layer Hen - Red Book.* [Online]
Available at: http://www.hyline.com/aspx/redbook/redbook.aspx?s=6&p=53
[Accessed 19 August 2014].

Leeson, S., 2009. *Future developments in poultry nutrition.* [Online]
Available at: http://www.thepoultrysite.com/articles/1381/future-developments-in-poultry-nutrition
[Accessed 19 August 2014].

Leeson, S. & Summers, J. D., 2012. *Commercial Poultry Nutrition.* 3rd ed. Ontario: Context Products Ltd.

Mississippi State University Extension Service, unknown. *Culling Hens.* [Online]
Available at: http://extension.msstate.edu/content/culling-hens
[Accessed 2017].

NSW Food Authority, 2017. *Egg Cleaning Procedures.* [Online]
Available at:
http://www.foodauthority.nsw.gov.au/_Documents/industry/egg_cleaning_procedures.pdf
[Accessed Jan 2017].

Olver, M. D. & Malan, D. D., 2000. The effect of choice feeding from 7 weeks of age on the production characteristics of laying hens. *South African Journal of Animal Science,* 2(30).

Poultry Hub, 2017. *Nutrient requirements of egg laying chcikens.* [Online]
Available at: http://www.poultryhub.org/nutrition/nutrient-requirements/nutrient-requirements-of-egg-laying-chickens/
[Accessed Jan 2017].

Poultry Pro, 2010. *Poultry Pro.* [Online]
Available at: http://www.poultrypro.com/poultry-articles/layers/feeding-programs-for-laying-hens-phase-feeding/
[Accessed 19 August 2014].

Scanes, C. G., Brant, G. & Ensminger, M. E., 2004. *Poultry Science.* 4th ed. s.l.:Stephen Helba.

The Merck Veterinary Manual, 2014. *Nutritional Requirements of Poultry.* [Online]
Available at:
http://www.merckmanuals.com/vet/poultry/nutrition_and_management_po

ultry/nutritional_requirements_of_poultry.html
[Accessed 19 August 2014].

The Poultry Hub, 2014. *Nutrient requirements of egg laying chickens.* [Online]
Available at: http://www.poultryhub.org/nutrition/nutrient-requirements/nutrient-requirements-of-egg-laying-chickens/
[Accessed 19 August 2014].

Wistedt, A., Ridderstrale, Y., Wall, H. & Holm, L., 2014. Exogenous estradiol improves shell strength in laying hens at the end of the laying period. *ACTA Veterinaria Scandinavica,* 56(34).